Richard Green Moulton

Four Years of Novel Reading

An account of an experiment in popularizing the study of fiction

Richard Green Moulton

Four Years of Novel Reading
An account of an experiment in popularizing the study of fiction

ISBN/EAN: 9783337049140

Printed in Europe, USA, Canada, Australia, Japan

Cover: Foto ©Thomas Meinert / pixelio.de

More available books at **www.hansebooks.com**

FOUR YEARS OF NOVEL READING: AN ACCOUNT OF AN EXPERIMENT IN POPULARIZING THE STUDY OF FICTION

EDITED, WITH AN INTRODUCTION, BY RICHARD G. MOULTON, M.A., PH.D. PROFESSOR OF LITERATURE IN ENGLISH IN THE UNIVERSITY OF CHICAGO

BOSTON, U.S.A.
D. C. HEATH & CO., PUBLISHERS
1895

COPYRIGHT, 1895,
BY R. G. MOULTON.

ELECTROTYPING BY C. J. PETERS & SON, BOSTON, U.S.A.

PRESSWORK BY S. J. PARKHILL & CO.

CONTENTS

INTRODUCTION: The Study of Fiction 1
    By PROFESSOR R. G. MOULTON.

THE "BACKWORTH CLASSICAL NOVEL-READING UNION" . 17
    By its Secretary, MR. JOHN U. BARROW.

FOUR YEARS' WORK DONE BY THE UNION 29

REPRESENTATIVE ESSAYS : —

    WHY IS CHARLES DICKENS A MORE FAMOUS NOVELIST
    THAN CHARLES READE ? 43
        By MISS ELLEN CUMPSTON.

    THE CHARACTER OF CLARA MIDDLETON 59
        By MR. JOSEPH FAIRNEY.

    THE IDEAL OF ASCETICISM 75
        By the REV. C. G. HALL.

    CHARACTER DEVELOPMENT IN "ROMOLA" 91
        By MR. THOMAS DAWSON.

INTRODUCTION

THE STUDY OF FICTION

FICTION may be described at the present time as just succeeding in living down a prejudice. It is now looked upon as a worldly and frivolous thing. But the time has been when it would have been accounted by many to be sinful. Most of us are old enough to recollect the time when a schoolboy would have his stock of storybooks confiscated by his teacher, while a schoolgirl might find herself sent to bed for the offence of being caught with a novel. Now our graver moralists go no farther than an affectionate warning: they will not condemn fiction, they will not judge others; but if their young friend wishes to make the best use of his time he will leave novel-reading to the idle, and restrict himself to literature founded on fact. I am afraid that if I were called upon for an affectionate warning, it would run the other way. It is good to make our reading catholic; but if my young friend be straitened in leisure and opportunity, I would counsel him to leave to more fortunate persons the literature that limits itself by fact, and make the best of his time by going straight to the world's great fiction.

If ever there might have been doubt about such counsel, it has ceased to be doubtful in the present day. Our great masters of the novel have been legion: from Miss Edgeworth and Jane Austen to George Eliot, Dickens, Thackeray, Reade, Kingsley, not to speak of the crowd of living novelists, some of whose masterpieces will not yield in rank even to the works of the greatest masters. Of the trinity who make the *Dii Majores* of our modern epoch, Tennyson deals largely with fiction; Browning's way is to weave a fictitious atmosphere about a mere kernel of fact; while William Morris — our English Homer — throws his whole literary message into the form of story. A similar predominance of fiction may be asserted of French and German literatures, so far as those literatures are read outside their native countries. And Russia is being admitted into the circle of great literary powers mainly on the strength of its novels. In such an age of fiction a vow of total abstinence is equivalent to a sentence of excommunication from contact with the best minds.

If we turn to the literature of the past, serious or light, it will appear that universality is more readily obtained by fictitious form than by any other device. The wisdom of primitive life has nearly all perished; that which has been kept alive has for the most part the form of fables and legends. In the great ages, what name is more suggestive of literary dignity than the name of Plato? Yet Plato has presented his whole

INTRODUCTION.

philosophy in a fictitious setting, — imaginary dialogues in which the characters, plot, and movement are as carefully elaborated as in an epic or drama. Higher authority yet may be quoted. Of the world's greatest Teacher, the one point of literary form which most impressed his contemporaries was his preference for fiction. "Without a parable spake he not unto them."

Whence, then, has arisen the strong prejudice of our fathers against novels, and the fainter echo of it by our graver moralists of to-day; while those who read fiction half apologize for what they put forward only as a relaxation or venial indulgence?

There is a certain tell-tale phrase that usually comes up in discussions of the subject, — fiction is contemptible because it is all "made up." Has not real life, we are asked, difficulties enough and sorrows of its own, without our needing to waste our tears on manufactured misery, or give precious time to persons and incidents which we know all the time never existed, but have been "made up" by a writer all out of his own head?

Fiction is objectionable, then, because it is "made up." Now, those who object most strongly are profound admirers of physical science. But are not the experiments of the man of science all "made up"? and does not their whole value consist in the fact that they are artificial substitutes of the investigator or expositor for actualities of nature that could not serve his purpose? We are to be taught the behavior of two gases when they meet. If our teacher is to be limited to the phenomena as they actually are found in nature, he must convey his audience perhaps to the bottom of the sea, or the interior of a floating cloud; when he has got them there the process in question is so intermingled with other processes that none but the trained observer could tell what was going on. Instead of this he "makes up" an experiment. He fetches each of the gases away from all that in actual nature would surround them; he locks them up, most unnaturally, in separate retorts until he is ready; instead of waiting for a real change of weather, he most artificially brings them together by a spark from a manufactured battery; and in an instant a truth is grasped by the simplest student which the cumbrous and involved processes of unassisted nature would have taken years to demonstrate, and even in years demonstrated only to the skilled observer.

Now, fiction is the experimental side of human science. Literature, we know, is the criticism of life. But such branches of literature as history and biography are at a disadvantage, because they must, like the mere observer of physical nature, confine their critical survey to what has actually happened. The poet and novelist can go far beyond this. They can reach the very heart of things by contriving human experiments; setting up, however artificially, the exact conditions and surroundings that will give a vital clearness to their truth. Physical science stood still for ages while its method was limited to actual observation of nature; it commenced its rapid advance when modern times invented the idea of experiment. It is similarly not surprising that the literature of humanity should have failed to make itself felt upon the modern mind while directors of education granted dignity only to the records of fact. When education begins to give proper prominence to the experimental exposition of life which we call fiction, the humanities may be expected to spring forward to an equality with the best-equipped sciences and philosophies.

It may be said boldly that *fiction is truer than fact*. Half the difference of opinion on the whole subject rests upon a mental confusion between the two things, fact and truth — fact, the mass of particular and individual details; truth, that is of general and universal import — fact, the raw material; truth, the finished article into which it is to be made up, with hundreds of chances of flaws in the working. Place side by side a biography of John Smith and a biographic novel like *Daniel Deronda* or *John Inglesant:* the novel will be "truer" than the biography, in the sense that it will contain more of "truth." However great and worthy John Smith may be, his life must include a large proportion of what is accidental, special to the individual.

The biography must insert this because its fidelity is to the facts. But a George Eliot has no motive for introducing anything that is not of general and universal significance. The biography will be the ore as it comes from the mine, gold and alloy mixed; the novel will be pure gold. Even this is an understatement of the case. The hero of the novel is not an individual at all, but the type of a whole class; not only will there be nothing accidental in the portrait, but in this one figure will be concentrated the essence of a hundred Daniel Derondas. The biography is the single specimen, and its gold is diluted with three times its weight of alloy; the truer novel is gold only, and gold from a hundred mines.

This contention that fiction is truer than fact will be called a paradox. But it is none the worse for that: a paradox is simply a truth standing on tiptoe to make itself seen; once recognized, the truth may descend to plain statement. Stripped of paradoxical form our principle comes to this: fiction is truer — or falser — than fact, but in any case more potent. Exposition by experiment may move along false lines, and buttress false theories. To handle facts is to look through plain glass, a mere transparent medium. Fiction is a lens that will concentrate, and the resultant picture will be attractive or repellent according as the lens is turned upon a landscape or a slum. Fiction will not lose its power to emphasize when it addresses itself to undesirable matter. On the other hand, the literature of fact is always limited in impressiveness, without any compensating immunity from error.

It is just here that another school of objectors make their stand. They recognize to the fullest degree the force of fiction, but lament that in our actual social life fiction is a force for evil. And they think the case can be met by warning against bad fiction; or at least by seeking to form a list of the ten or the hundred Best Novels, so that a natural appetite for fiction may be harmlessly gratified.

With the basis of fact on which this position is grounded it is impossible not to sympathize. The vast proportion of the novel-reading that actually goes on in our midst has no title to the present defence of fiction. If we analyze it, it will seem to be, to a great extent, the intrusion of the universal gambling spirit into literature. What betting or euchre are to the men's club, that novels are to the ladies' boudoir. The pleasure of gambling lies in an intoxicating prolongation of uncertainty in a matter where there is interest without the power of control. So what gets the typical novel read is the long-drawn-out uncertainty whether Clarissa is to be married or buried in the last chapter, with a delicious off-chance (if Mr. Hardy be the novelist) that she may even come to be hanged. The matter admits of an easy test — what percentage of our novel-readers have ever read a novel twice? We all want to see a good picture ten times and more; those to whom fiction is one of the fine arts will be able to produce their list of stories read five, six, ten times. The value of a novel increases with the square of the number of times it has been read.

Or, again, a good deal of novel-reading is literary gossip and literary fashion. The elegant among us will read, not only stories, but the reviews of them; apparently not for the purpose for which reviews exist, but from the strange fascination that possesses many minds for catching up something that somebody says about some work, and quickly passing it on, not only without thinking about the remark, but without the least idea of reading the work to which it refers. Current fiction stands second only to social scandal as material for flying gossip. Others are impelled by an anxiety to be up to date. Just as in dress or house arrangement they buy things, not because they are good, nor for the excellent reason that they like them, but mainly because they are the fashion, so they will blush to confess that they have not read *Dodo*, while feeling no discomfort at not having read Dante.

Readers who suspect in themselves infirmities of this kind in their attitude to fiction should prescribe to themselves a self-denying ordinance by which they should read nothing that is not ten years old. In such a practice they would find a sifting machinery stronger than a host of reviews.

Our objectors are right, then, in their facts, but wrong, surely, in the remedy they think to apply. Education by *Index Expurgatorius* has never succeeded. The institution of Novels Laureate, we may be sure, would make little headway against the keen pleasure of free choice. It is a case for reform; but the change needs to be made, not in the books, but in the readers.

The practical issue to which these considerations lead up is that taste in fiction needs training. The literature of fact is easy; all creative art involves a receptivity prepared by cultivation. Two men are seated side by side on a promenade, listening to the music of the band. To the one there is no difference between the popular polka and the adagio from a Beethoven symphony; they are simply successive items in an evening's entertainment. To the man seated by him, the two pieces are wide as the poles asunder; the one gives a moment's amusement, by the other his whole soul is called out, and he feels himself in converse with giants of the world of mind. Yet the music was the same for both hearers; the difference was made by the training of the ear. Cultivation does the same for fiction. The very novel that one man reads to keep off ennui till dinner shall be ready, when read by another, and a trained reader, fills his soul with a sense of artistic beauty, and makes him long to be good. If novel-reading, taken as a whole, has been a curse rather than a blessing, the fault lies, not in our authors, but in our distorted educational system, which insists upon careful training in mathematics, or language, or physical science, — subjects comparatively easy and remote from life, — yet leaves literature, most difficult and vital of all studies, to take care of itself. In this matter, surely, we may take our moral censors with us. Fiction is going to be read, whether they like it or not; but they may attain the object at which they are really aiming, if they turn their energy into the channel of demanding that preliminary training which will determine whether fiction shall be a dissipation or a mental and moral food.

But how is this cultivation to be attained? Not, surely, by the reading of reviews. Who could think of getting an ear for music by reading reports of concerts in the musical columns of the press? We know we can be trained in music only by hearing the music itself. Taste in fiction can be cultivated only by reading and re-reading the works of the great masters, with docile attention always, and sometimes with distinct effort and study. I am not speaking of the professed student, with leisure and means to use the machinery of university education to assist him in developing his receptive powers. But the busy men and women, to whom literature can never be anything else than recreation, may make their recreation productive, if they are willing to invest in it a little of the mental capital we call study. The practical problem is to find modes of studying fiction such as will fit themselves into the routine of ordinary busy life.

The object of the present book is to introduce a little experiment that has been made in this matter of popularizing the study of fiction. It has been tried in a mining village of Northumbérland (England), and in spite of limitations of leisure and social opportunity it has flourished long enough to present "four years of novel-reading." The pages that follow will speak for themselves; here it is enough to say, that the plan consists in the reading, by all the members of this "Classical Novel-Reading Union," of the same novel at the same period, while the announcement of the novel to be read is accompanied with suggestions, coming from some "literary authority," of some one or two "points to be noted" in the book. The scheme includes meetings for discussing the novel and reading essays; but its essence lies in the two things I have mentioned, — simultaneous reading, and reading in the light of an expert's suggestions as to important points. The history of this novel-reading union is sketched below by its secretary, and a record follows of the work done. It cannot but be interesting to note the works selected, the ideas they have called out, and especially the suggestions made by those who have been consulted as literary authorities.

It is interesting, again, to note that this list of literary authorities includes, not only local friends, or those whose work is education, but sometimes novelists of such rank as Mr. Justin McCarthy, Miss Peard, and the author of *John Inglesant*. A few representative essays are added, selected from those read at meetings of the Union. They reflect only the opinions of the individual writers; but they will add to the general interest of the present volume.

The reader will understand that what is here introduced is not put forward as a model method of studying fiction. It is too early to talk of models; fiction-study is in the tentative stage, and only experiment is possible; what is here done is to record an experiment. It is an experiment that can be tried on a larger scale by the formation of similar unions, or on a smaller scale by a few friends reading together; while isolated readers can join this or similar societies at a distance, and gain the major part of the advantages of the plan. Without going farther, the four years' experience here presented will afford a not inconsiderable training in novel-reading to any who may try to follow it. I will add, that if any readers of these pages are induced to try for themselves the plan here described, or any other plan suggested by it, and would find some means of making public their experience in the matter, they would be doing good service in helping towards that comparison of experiments which leads up to the survival of the fittest method. Whether it be by the union of several students in a society, or by the individual efforts of isolated readers, in some way the regular study of fiction must be set on foot. And this study of fiction will be, in its highest form, the study of life.

R. G. MOULTON.

FOUR YEARS OF NOVEL-READING

THE BACKWORTH
CLASSICAL NOVEL-READING UNION

BACKWORTH
CLASSICAL NOVEL-READING UNION

A BRIEF HISTORY

BACKWORTH forms part of a group of mining villages lying near to a north-eastern headland of the German Ocean, and is one of the many small industrial centres spreading like net-work throughout the great mining county of Northumberland. If any evidence were required of the immense improvement in industrial conditions, and of the general progress of the mining class, in this part of England, it would only be necessary to contrast Backworth with some of the older mining villages, decaying remnants of which are to be found, where active industry is no longer in progress. Its improved dwellings, commodious board schools, flourishing co-operative society, popular workmen's institute, and a number of other interests and advantages, are so many proofs of its general prosperity and happiness as compared with the life and conditions prevailing in mining communities thirty years ago.

When the great movement of University Extension

was conceived and began its benignant career, it was almost natural that its earliest missionaries should find their way to Northumberland. Backworth, with many other places, associated itself with the scheme in these early days; but to Backworth alone belongs the distinction of having maintained an almost unbroken attachment for many years. It was during a course of University Extension lectures that the movement to which this brief history relates first took definite shape, and the "Classical Novel-Reading Union" had its birth.

The first course of lectures of a purely literary nature was delivered in the spring of 1890, and among other lessons taught was the importance of fiction as a wholesome and educational influence. It was soon discovered that although Backworth read fiction, it was not fiction of the best class; and there was no systematic study of the best works of the best authors, and scanty knowledge of the great classics of fiction which are among life's best text-books. This course of lectures was one of the most successful ever held in Backworth. It was followed by deep and intelligent interest, and awoke in many the first perceptions of the great educational value of literature; and when it was suggested that a society should be formed, the object of which should be the study of classical fiction, the project was received with an appreciation closely allied to enthusiasm.

The idea having been adopted, the principle, purpose,

and plan of operation of the proposed society, were embodied in a circular as follows:—

PRINCIPLE.

Literature is the science of life; and the great classical novels are among the best text-books of life. To study these is the true antidote to trashy and poisonous fiction.

PURPOSE.

The purpose of the Union is to encourage a course of systematic novel-reading, (1) at the rate of a novel a month; (2) to be taken up by ordinary readers and students, the former reading and talking about the novels, the latter meeting to discuss and do work.

PLAN OF OPERATION.

1. A post-card will be sent to every member at the beginning of the month announcing, (*a*) the novel chosen for the month; (*b*) a very brief suggestion from some competent literary authority of some leading points to be kept in view during the reading of the work; (*c*) the date and business of the first meeting.

2. All joining the Union undertake to read during the month the novel selected, and from time to time endeavor to turn conversation upon it.

3. All members are invited to attend, and (if they like) take part in the meetings of the Union. At the same time it is fully recognized that many more will undertake the reading than those able to attend the meetings or do work.

4. The business of the meetings will be, (1) the reading and discussion of papers (especially upon subjects connected with the suggestions made by the

literary authority); (2) discussion of difficulties or queries started by members; or (3) formal debates upon questions arising out of the novel of the month.

5. There will be one meeting in the earlier half of each month; others during the month (if found desirable), by adjournment from the first, or by the appointment of the council. If practicable, meetings shall be held in various places in the district.

MEMBERSHIP AND GOVERNMENT.

1. The membership shall include local and distant members, the only pledge required being that they shall read the book selected for the month.

2. The Union to be governed by a president, vice-presidents, secretary, and a council of six, to be elected annually.

The chief duty of the latter shall be the selection of novels, and general oversight in the work of the Union.

These circulars were distributed throughout the district prior to the last lecture of the course, at which it was announced that a supply of post-cards had been provided, by which intending members might notify the secretary of their desire to become members of the "Backworth and District Classical Novel-Reading Union." Three weeks from the date of this meeting the membership stood at forty-six; and with this number a start was made with the first novel for the month of May. The chief agent of the colliery undertook the presidency, a number of gentlemen — including the two parliamentary representatives of the miners — accepted the vice-presidency, and a representative council was elected to control the business of the society. The room of the local Students' Association was selected as the place of meeting, and the printing of post-cards, etc., was to be done with a small hand printing-press, the property of the same body. A list of six novelists was drawn up, — Dickens, Thackeray, Scott, Kingsley, Lytton, and "George Eliot;" and the secretary was instructed to make application to competent literary authorities for suggestions or "points to be noted" in any work of these authors. Dickens's *Martin Chuzzlewit* was the first book read by the Union, and fully bore out the interest anticipated in the formation of the society.

During the months which ensued, additions were steadily made to the membership, until in six months it had reached eighty-seven, nearly double the number at the beginning. These were not entirely local members. The local press had published accounts of the formation of the Union, and induced many living at a distance to make application for membership; and about one-third of the membership at this time was drawn from persons living at a distance. It was urged that local unions might be formed by these in their own districts; but it was felt that the experience of the first year of the Backworth enterprise might be useful before steps were taken in this direction.

And now, with a few months' experience, weak places

were discovered in the general plan of operation, and these finally developed into considerable difficulties.

Three main points were brought up for the consideration of a special meeting:—

1. It was felt that a month was too short a time to read the novels thoroughly.
2. Literary authorities did not respond readily.
3. Members were unwilling to commit themselves to do any work until they had read the book, and thus essays and debates did not prosper.

At this specially convened meeting the following amendments were made to the constitution:—

1. Two months was to be the time allotted for reading the novel.
2. University Extension lecturers were to be added to the list of literary authorities.
3. A meeting was to be held at the end of the first month for the arrangement of essays, debates, etc., when it was hoped that members having some knowledge of the book would feel themselves more competent to undertake the work.

These changes no doubt represent a very considerable departure from the original plan of the Union, but it is only necessary to point out that they in no way interfered with the principle of the society. The earlier plan was necessarily tentative; and from the fact that the scheme originated in a mining district, with all its busy interests, and consequently limited leisure for the purposes of the Union, any adaptation to meet local requirements does not presume want of success. For a district with more leisure, a wider acquaintance with books, and greater educational facilities, the original plan is worthy of consideration, and would no doubt be practicable, and for this reason has been included *in extenso* in these notes. Backworth, however, found the change beneficial, and the society exists on these lines to-day. The longer time allotted gives greater opportunity for *thorough* reading. Literary suggestions are more easily obtained from those who know or have heard of Backworth as a successful University Extension centre. And the knowledge obtained in the first month's reading enables members to undertake definite work in the shape of an essay, or the negative or affirmative in a debate.

From the date of the acceptance of these changes in the constitution and administration of the Union progress has been slow, but certain. It was inevitable that some should enter the society with mistaken views as to its object and purpose, with nothing more than a curious interest in its actual working, and with little or no sympathy for the definite principles of the society. Like the poor, these are always with us. But although our increase has been largely discounted by a corresponding decrease due to a variety of causes (personal and local), and by the process of weeding out those indifferent to the pledge of membership, we have been able to maintain a sound body of members numbering eighty-three, that are in full sympathy with the objects of the institution, and faithful to its pledge and purpose. A uniform subscription of one shilling per member, payable on entrance, is sufficient to meet all the expenses of the Union. Members provide their own books, either by loan or purchase; or sometimes, in the case of a group of students, by mutual purchase — each member obtaining the use of the book in turn, while it is finally disposed of to the members in rotation.

At the end of the first month an informal discussion takes place on the points to be noted, and subjects are set for essay and debate. The latter are not always accepted, members selecting their subjects according to their individual tastes, but always with due regard to the particular book under discussion. Occasionally papers are given at this meeting, which might be called supplementary papers, as they often deal with subjects previously discussed, and are brought forward when a debate or essay has not covered the whole subject from the writer's point of view. Distant members contribute papers to the general meeting, and at their own request have the papers of local members sent to them. With a larger society, and special means at our command, every member would be provided with a copy, or at least a *précis*, of the proceedings at the general meeting.

An annual report is issued by the secretary, in which

membership, work done, finance, and future prospects are discussed; and each member is supplied with a copy of this report, from which may be gathered the general progress of the society.

This is a brief outline of the "Novel-Reading Union" as it at present exists; and some idea of its work and usefulness may be seen in the following table:—

Books Read	20
Papers Given . . .	54
Meetings Held	34

The list of authors has been extended, taking in Victor Hugo, Charles Reade, George Meredith, Mrs. Gaskell, Eugène Sue, Charlotte Bronté, etc.; and the great works of these great authors have been a constant source of pleasure to those privileged to read them under the guidance of skilled literary advisers. Nor has the work been one of pleasure alone. The avowed principle upon which the Union is based is to make fiction, which contains some of the best thinking of the age, not only a pleasant, but an educational pursuit; to neutralize the trashy and pernicious literature which abounds in these days of cheap books, and to train earnest students, not only in the best thought, but in the literary ways and methods of the best novelists. It is sometimes urged against our scheme, that it deals only with one department of literature to the exclusion of others equally interesting, and possibly more profitable. The use of this argument implies forgetfulness of the root idea of the Union. It does not concern itself with the literary tastes of members, except in so far as these tastes incline to fiction. We assume that fiction has some place in the reading of every one who reads at all. We fix this occasional reading at the rate of a novel in two months, and ask that the reading be systematically done, and educational in purpose. It is no part of our plan to provide pleasure without profit, and it cannot be too clearly emphasized that the Union is not merely a recreative organization.

One remark may be added. It has constantly been urged upon us from outside, that our local effort would be a service to literary study in general, because it would be pioneering with a view to discover a practical method of systematically studying fiction, which, when once discovered and tested by experience, would probably be adopted elsewhere. This has been done at such places as London and Exeter; and a further result of this local effort may be seen in the larger place given to fiction in the programmes of the numerous debating societies, in both town and country, and in the general consent which has been accorded to the idea that the importance of the novel as a vehicle of thought, and its influence in life, are such as to justify special study and organization.

J. U. BARROW.

FOUR YEARS' WORK

DONE BY

THE BACKWORTH CLASSICAL NOVEL-READING UNION

WORK DONE BY THE C. N. R. U.

FIRST NOVEL

Martin Chuzzlewit, by Charles Dickens.

Points to be noted (suggested by Prof. R. G. Moulton).
1. Four different types of selfishness, — Old Martin, Young Martin, Antony, and Pecksniff.
2. Four different types of unselfishness, — Mary, Mark Tapley, Old Chuffey, and Tom Pinch.

Debate. — That the two swindles in the story (Scadder's Land Office and the English Insurance Company) are inconceivable.

Essays.
1. Is Mark Tapley's character overdrawn?
2. Changes in the characters of the book from Selfishness to Unselfishness.

Difficulty Raised. — How could Tom Pinch go so long undeceived in Pecksniff?

SECOND NOVEL

Anne of Geierstein, by Sir Walter Scott.

Point to be noted (suggested by Prof. R. G. Moulton).
The supernatural element in the story; how much is intended to be real? how much self-deception? how much imposture?

Debate. — Was the Vehme-Gericht, as described by Scott, a righteous institution?

Essay. — The character of Burgundy as painted in another novel of Scott's.

Difficulty Raised. — How could such daughters come of such fathers — as Anne and Queen Margaret, of Count Albert and King Réné?

THIRD NOVEL
A Tale of Two Cities, by Charles Dickens
Point to be noted (suggested by Justin McCarthy, Esq., M.P.).

The author's description of a French mob in this novel contrasted with his description of an English mob in *Barnaby Rudge*.

Debate. — Was the noble self-sacrifice of the hero within the range of human generosity?

Essay. — The character of Carton as it develops under the influence of his pure, unselfish love.

FOURTH NOVEL
Westward-Ho! by Charles Kingsley.
Point to be noted (suggested by Prof. R. G. Moulton).

Character contrasts in the same family (a study of the two brothers Leigh and their cousin Eustace).

Debate. — The morality of the English expeditions against the West.

FIFTH NOVEL
Ninety-Three, by Victor Hugo.
Points to be noted (suggested by A. J. Grant, Esq., M.A.).
1. That the book is without any important female character. How is the interest sustained without it?
2. Does the story strike you as characteristically French, and in what respects?
3. The character of the Marquis de Latenac as representing the best side of the ancient *régime*.

Debate. — Was Cimourdain right in condemning Gauvain to death?

Essay. — Victor Hugo's view of the Revolution.

SIXTH NOVEL
Vanity Fair, by Wm. M. Thackeray.
Points to be noted (suggested by Prof. O. Seaman).
1. Worldliness absorbs the art and charm of the novel. Becky at the worst nearly always fascinates. Virtue is made

either dull or absurd. Amelia is a poor hysterical thing, and worships a snob. Lady Jane is a good-natured nonentity, and loves a prig. Dobbin, the *real* hero, has large feet, and is generally awkward. Religion is made synonymous with cant.
2. Note two kinds of vulgarity in the attitude of the middle classes toward the aristocracy, — (*a*) a fawning admiration, as shown by many of the characters; (*b*) an affectation of contempt, as shown constantly by the author himself.
3. The delightful balance of interest is due to Thackeray's power of reticence as well as of expression. Waterloo, for instance, is not made an excuse for fine writing or protracted description. The single line that tells of George Osborne's death is a stroke of art.

Character Sketch. — Captain Dobbin.

Debate. — Was Rawdon Crawley justified in condemning his wife?

Essay. — The redeeming qualities in Becky Sharp.

SEVENTH NOVEL

Put Yourself in His Place, by Charles Reade.

Points to be noted (suggested by Miss Spence).
1. Three main purposes of the author: (*a*) to show that in the struggle of capital and labor due consideration has not been given to the value of life; (*b*) the power of sympathy as an interpreter of the actions of others; (*c*) the cowardly and inhuman methods trade unions have resorted to.
2. That the interest of character is quite subordinate to that of incident. The dramatic and picturesque character of some of the situations: viz., the turning of the portrait in the hall at Raby; scene in the old church during a snow-storm.

Debate. — Was Simmons right to keep silence on his death-bed?

Essay. — The legitimate scope of trade unions.

EIGHTH NOVEL

Silas Marner, by George Eliot.

Points to be noted (suggested by G. L. Dickinson, Esq., M.A.).

1. Note the gradual disappearance of village life such as that described in the book before improved communications, large factories, etc.
2. The change in Silas Marner's character under the influence of the child he has adopted. This is the central motive of the book.
3. The nemesis falling on Godfrey in his childlessness by his wife, while all the time his illegitimate child is growing up near him, but unknown to him.

Debate. — Is the effect of large industry an advantage or a disadvantage to human and social relations?

Essay. — Nemesis.

NINTH NOVEL

Jane Eyre, by Charlotte Brontë.

Points to be noted (suggested by Dr. A. S. Percival).

1. The book is neither artistic nor realistic, yet it possesses an engrossing interest. On what does the interest depend?
2. The characters:—

    Jane Eyre, a woman of little human sympathy, upright by rule rather than from any impulsive love of right. Note the vulgarity of her distrust of Rochester during her engagement.

    Rochester, a woman's false type of manliness. He has a certain nobility, though his roughness and coarseness detract from the strength of his character.

    St. John Rivers, a selfish prig; his uprightness based purely on hope of future reward.

Debate. — Can Rochester's conduct to Jane Eyre be justified?

Essay. — The character of the author as revealed in the book.

TENTH NOVEL

Wives and Daughters, by Mrs. Gaskell.

Points to be noted (suggested by Miss Peard).

1. Note especially with what subtlety the laws of heredity are shown to work in the characters of Mrs. Gibson and Molly, Mrs. Gibson and Cynthia, the Squire and Mrs. Hamley, and their two sons; the modification or accentuation of certain traits in the children.
2. The charm of truthfulness and absence of exaggeration in the book.

Debate. — Was cowardice the moral failing which worked most mischief in the course of the story?

Essay. — The law of heredity as shown in various characters in the book.

ELEVENTH NOVEL

Romola, by George Eliot.

Points to be noted (suggested by W. E. Norris, Esq.).

It is to the study of Tito Melema in chief that *Romola* — excellent as the work is throughout — owes its immortality. Note especially how his selfishness and cowardice have to be indicated so early in the book, that the reader's sympathies are necessarily alienated from him, and it is therefore all the greater triumph on the writer's part to have conveyed the impression that in real life his charm would have been almost irresistible. To have discovered something about the methods by which this character has been made to stand upon his feet is, no doubt, to have discovered something about the technical side of light literature.

Essays.

1. The character of Savonarola, and the secret of his influence.
2. Tito and Romola: a contrast.
3. Tito: as a political study, and a work of art.

TWELFTH NOVEL

Persuasion, by Jane Austen.

Points to be noted (suggested by J. H. Shorthouse, Esq.).

1. The extraordinary vitality of Miss Austen's characters, the more surprising as they are all, or nearly all, commonplace and ordinary people.
2. The character of Anne Elliot (considered by some to be the most perfect piece of work in English fiction).

Debate. — Was Anne Elliot self-conscious? and, if so, is self-consciousness a fault? and why?

THIRTEENTH NOVEL

Alton Locke, by Charles Kingsley.

Points to be noted (suggested by Arthur Berry, Esq., M.A.).

1. This is essentially a novel with a purpose; namely, to raise public opinion against the evils of sweating, to denounce cheapness and competition, and to advocate the union of the gentry and clergy with the working-classes against the commercial classes.
2. Note the evil influence of Lillian on Alton.
3. The character of Sandy Mackaye.

Essay. — Whether it is good art to teach political or other doctrines in a novel.

Debate. — Is the conversion of Alton natural?

Essay. — Literary symbolism (Sandy Mackaye — Thomas Carlyle).

FOURTEENTH NOVEL

Kenilworth, by Sir Walter Scott.

Points to be noted (suggested by Mr. Thomas Dawson).

1. Note how the general interest of the book is wonderfully divided between the narrative and the graphic pictures of English life in the Elizabethan period. Compare and contrast these pictures with those drawn in *Westward Ho!*

2. Note the character of Queen Elizabeth, especially when she frequently betrays the weakness of her sex.
3. It is not until the honor of Amy Robsart is imperilled that the real strength and nobility of her character is discovered.
4. Observe the mesmeric power possessed by Varney, especially in the scene when Amy drinks the liquid offered by him.

Debate. — Which is the greater villain — Varney or Foster?

Essay. — The literary use of mesmeric fascination.

FIFTEENTH NOVEL

The Wandering Jew, by Eugène Sue.

Points to be noted (suggested by Prof. R. G. Moulton).
1. Note how the legendary immortality of an individual is brought into contact with immortality as seen (1) in a family, (2) in property — compound interest, (3) in a corporation — the Jesuits.
2. Contrast the first part of the book — intrigue by violent opposition — with the second part, — the intrigue that acts through the passions of its opponents.

Essays.
1. The difficulties and improbabilities of the story.
2. The legend of the Wandering Jew in literature.

SIXTEENTH NOVEL

The Cloister and the Hearth, by Charles Reade.

Points to be noted (suggested by G. L. Dickinson, Esq., M.A.).
1. The value of the historical novel as supplementing history, giving with vividness the manners and customs and daily life of the period.
2. The particular characteristics of the period with which the novel deals, — the transition from the Middle Ages to the Renaissance.
3. The main interest of the story proper is the way in which the love of Gerard and Margaret is transformed without

being lessened when they are unable to live as husband and wife.
4. The broad humanity of the author, as, for example, in his sympathetic treatment of the soldier Denys, and of the beggar with whom Gerard travels.

Essay. — The ideal of asceticism.

SEVENTEENTH NOVEL

Esmond, by Wm. M. Thackeray.

Points to be noted (suggested by Miss Peard).
1. Note the absence of any great central situation in *Esmond*. There is scarcely one striking incident which takes hold of the reader, whereas the characters remain strong and distinct in the memory.
2. Note the excellence of the style. The story is told with extreme vigor and directness, and there is nothing which can be called ornamental description. Yet no historical novel carries one so completely into the spirit of the age.

Debate. — Is Thackeray a cynic, or a great moral satirist?

Essay. — The characters of Thackeray.

EIGHTEENTH NOVEL

The Egoist. by George Meredith.

Points to be noted (suggested by E. Saltmarshe, Esq.).
1. Note the descriptions of nature.
2. The intensely pathetic figure of the hero.
3. The restrained humor in "the aged and great wine scene."

Debate. — Eliminating the chance which broke off the engagement, had Clara Middleton force of character enough to win her freedom again, having made the resolution to do so, or would Sir Willoughby, with the powerful conventional weapon she had given him, viz., her plighted troth, backed by his endless resource of sophistry, and the subterfuges to which his egoism was capable of sending him, have won the day?

Essay. — The methods and teaching of George Meredith.

WORK DONE BY THE C. N. R. U. 37

NINETEENTH NOVEL

David Copperfield, by Charles Dickens.

Points to be noted (suggested by Sir Courtenay Boyle, K.C.B.).
1. How far was Mr. Micawber's improvidence personal to himself? and how far due to his surroundings? What is the possibility that in real life a change of scene would have led to the change of character hinted at in the novel?
2. What is there to admire in (*a*) Steerforth, (*b*) Peggotty, (*c*) Traddles?

Debate. — Does Dickens abuse literary art?

Essay. — David Copperfield as a prig.

TWENTIETH NOVEL

Elsie Venner, by O. W. Holmes.

Points to be noted (suggested by T. L. Brunton, Esq., M.D., F.R.S.).
1. Note the effect of inherited tendencies on the actions of individuals.
2. The effect of accidental circumstances (e.g., disease affecting a parent) on the character of the offspring.

Debate. — How far was Bernard Langdon justified in punishing Abner Briggs and his dog, considering that they were both acting according to their natures, which they had partly inherited from their ancestors, and which were partly developed by the circumstances in which they were brought up?

Essay. — How far is the character of Elsie Venner to be regarded as a description of fact? and how far as a parable?

TWENTY-FIRST NOVEL

Woodstock, by Sir Walter Scott.

Points to be noted (suggested by Stanley Wayman, Esq.).
1. The strange types of character produced by the troubles of the civil war: (1) Harrison, the religious fanatic. (2) Bletson, the philosophic atheist. (3) Desborough, the ignorant, ox-like man, wandering in the dark.

2. Three types of the king's party: (1) The old-fashioned punctilious royalist, Sir Henry Lee. (2) The gallant, high-bred cavalier, Albert Lee. (3) The reckless, dissolute cavalier, Wildrake.

Debate. — Is the character of Trusty Tompkins, the forcible preacher and the low spy and schemer, consistent or possible?

Essay. — The character of Cromwell as portrayed in *Woodstock*. Is it, so far as is now known, correct?

TWENTY-SECOND NOVEL

The Shadow of the Sword, by R. Buchanan.

Points to be noted (suggested by W. F. Moulton, Esq., M.A.).

Note especially the personality of Napoleon. "He is not a great man: he has no heart." Discuss this statement of Mr. Arfoll's.

Debate. — Does Robert Buchanan clear Gwenfern entirely of the imputation of cowardice?

Essay. — The ethics of war.

TWENTY-THIRD NOVEL

Lorna Doone, by R. D. Blackmore.

Points to be noted (suggested by E. J. Mathew, Esq., B.A.).

1. The plot. Simple in itself, and somewhat complicated in the manner of telling. This is done purposely, to throw some light on the character of John Ridd himself.

2. The local coloring of the book is excellent. It conveys a wonderfully accurate idea of Devonshire and Somerset. Many tales dealing with special localities are capital for those who already know those localities. *Lorna Doone* goes farther than this. Note also the racial hatreds between Celt and Saxon, especially when a Cornish person is introduced.

3. Note how carefully and consistently the characters are drawn; how each keeps its individuality throughout the book. Note especially the clever studies of woman. Mrs.

Ridd, the two sisters, Ruth Huckaback and Betty Muxworthy, being all really more complicated than Lorna herself.
4. Note the style of the book. The prose often has a wonderful rhythm and ordered movement about it, so that it sometimes comes to be almost blank verse. Also note the author's keen eye for color and effect in describing scenery.

Debate. — The nature of the book. Is it, or is it not, romantic?

Essay. — The character of John Ridd.

TWENTY-FOURTH NOVEL

Our Mutual Friend, by Charles Dickens.

Points to be noted (suggested by the Earl of Suffolk).
1. Note how greed will swamp and extinguish gratitude, as shown by Silas Wegg and Mr. Boffin, and the reverse as shown by the Boffins in their conduct to their late employer's son.
2. Note Dickens's view of the Poor Law, as illustrated in the life of Betty Higden.

Essay. — Dickens and Thackeray: a contrast.

Debate. — Was Harmon justified in concealing his identity after he knew of his supposed murder?

Difficulty Raised. — Is it possible for a man to be at the same time so shrewd and so unsuspicious as Mr. Boffin (always remembering his position in life) is represented to be?

TWENTY-FIFTH NOVEL

The Count of Monte Cristo, by Alexander Dumas.

Points to be noted (suggested by Prof. R. G. Moulton).
1. *The Count of Monte Cristo* is a masterpiece of the French school, especially suitable for the study of fiction from its many-sidedness. It is a terrible tragedy, an elaborate study of human nature and society; and in particular, it is a consummate piece of literary workmanship from beginning to end.

2. Note some of the details by which Dumas builds up a sense of mysterious and irresistible power as attaching to his hero.
3. Note the following personages considered as race-types: Fernand, Danglars, Mercédès, Haydée, Caderousse, Bertuccio, Faria, Vampa.
4. Note the retribution upon Villefort, Danglars, Fernand, and Caderousse.

Essays.
1. Trace in complete outline one of the main schemes of retribution in the story.
2. Show how Monte Cristo's sense of his mission as an Earthly Providence begins to give way.

ESSAYS

WHY IS CHARLES DICKENS A MORE FAMOUS NOVELIST THAN CHARLES READE?

WHY IS CHARLES DICKENS A MORE FAMOUS NOVELIST THAN CHARLES READE?

THE fact of Dickens's popularity is established beyond all question. Any one who doubts this has only to make investigation at any reference library to find, that, besides the various editions of Dickens's novels which meet the demands and resources of every class of people, there is a constantly increasing literature which has taken root and flourishes on every item of Dickens's life, habits, haunts, works, and philosophy.

Ask, on the other hand, for information about Reade, and you will meet with doubtful answers. A few incomplete notices of his life in biographical dictionaries will be shown you, the fact that he is dead will be insisted on, and you will be told that a sixpenny edition of his books is being published.

Yet Walter Besant, no mean novelist, places Reade at the head of his profession, and Algernon Charles Swinburne indorses and strengthens Besant's verdict. What that verdict is the subjoined quotations will show.

"If all English-speaking readers were to vote for the best of living novelists, there can be little doubt that they would name Charles Reade. I am one of those who would so vote. I entirely agree with the popular verdict. I, for one, consider that Reade takes rank with Fielding, Smollet, Scott, Dickens, and Thackeray; that is to say, in the great and delightful art of fiction, wherein the English — who are always, in every age, doing something better than their neighbors — have surpassed the world, Charles Reade stands among the foremost and best. . . . Let those who appreciate the best, the most faithful, the highest work in the Royal Art of Fiction, salute the Master." — WALTER BESANT in *The Gentleman*.

"He has left not a few pages which, if they do not live as long as the English language, will fail to do so through no fault of their own, but solely through the malice of accident, by which so many reputations worthy of a longer life have been casually submerged or eclipsed. . . . That he was at his very best, and that not very rarely, a truly great writer of a truly noble genius, I do not understand how any competent judge of letters could possibly hesitate to affirm." — ALGERNON CHARLES SWINBURNE.

These are valuable testimonials to the fame of any writer; but we have undertaken to prove that Reade's novels will never become classics, and to find out why in this respect they differ from those of Dickens. Classics may be roughly defined as being works which will live. The *Iliad* is a classic, so is the Bible, so is *La Divina Commedia*, so are *Æsop's Fables*. All these diverse books agree in three great essentials: they are written from the heart of man (not *a* man) to the heart of man; they are not in any prevailing fashion, which might become out of date, but in the chameleon garb of an ever-changing universe; and they were not written to make a book, or for any other reason than that the writers were thrilled by a touch on the cord that binds us to the highest and lowest in creation, and being so thrilled, had to pass on the mighty influence, whether it suited their momentary convenience or not. The live coal from off the altar of inspiration which has touched the lips of all our great classical writers has been as different as the lips it has touched. But it has always been burning with scorn of some fundamental sin of our race, not sputtering fitfully with party spites and parish cabals.

The knowledge of a worthy aim, and the consciousness of being a mouthpiece of what the Germans call the " Zeitgeist," gives a leisureliness, a grand even-paced march to the style of great writers, which is as different as possible from the forceless fretting of the small antagonist of local abuses. Let us fix firmly in our minds that, though vogue seems greater than fame at times, it is no more so in reality than a firework is brighter than the stars, or a fashionable song more enduring than a melody of Beethoven's.

Now, the above remarks apply, of course, only indirectly to novels, which are, as it were, merely the blossoms of literature. But, seeing that only one reader out of twenty makes any pretence of reading anything but fiction, it is necessary for connoisseurs of novel-reading to be able to distinguish a good novel from a bad one. Reduced to its elements, the judgment of a novel must go on the same lines as that of any other literary work; but, lest the definition we have supplied should seem inappropriate to such books as those we are considering, we will go into detail, and deal more with concrete examples.

All good things are in trinities; therefore again we demand three qualities in the novel we like to read. We demand firstly, that it shall not bore us; secondly, that it shall not bear the stamp of untruth on its face; and thirdly, that it shall leave us better men and women than it found us.

Now, applying our first standard of excellence to Reade's three best-known novels, we are compelled to confess that his company wearies us extremely. His characters are not alive, they never were, and we are too thankful to know that they never will be. In creating them he seems to have said to himself, "I want an innocent, pure-minded girl in this chapter," — or "I want a villain," — or "a comic doctor," as the case may be, and forthwith he turns his eye inward to see what his own idea of such an article is; then, without comparing his conception of it with the specimens around him, he drags out his material, and sticks it together, labels it "high-souled maiden," "honest, eccentric doctor," "fastidious matron," or "noble-minded man of

God," and hangs the incidents of his certainly clever plots upon the pegs so mechanically provided.

He is not content with this cataloguing of his people: he allows them each only one spring of action, and one method of expressing themselves. And yet with all this we have no mental picture of his personages before our eyes. His character sketches are not graphic, though his narrative is. If he had used half the knowledge and energy in telling about his humans that he has done in describing his storms, dangers, and accidents, he might have taken a much higher place than he has done amongst his brother writers.

After all, it is human nature most of us care to read about, human nature as acted on by this and that event; not events disconnected from their human surroundings, and forced into undue prominence by three black pencil marks, and a host of exclamation notes and changes of type, to attract our attention to them.

We might draw up a list of Reade's characters without difficulty, and it would stand thus:—

Prigs: Alfred Hardie, George Fielding, William Fielding, Frank Eden, the clergyman in *Foul Play* (whose name has escaped us), Mr. Saunders, etc.

Bashful maidens inclined to piety: Julia Dodd, Jane Hardie, Susan Merton, Christie Johnstone, and the heroine of *Foul Play*, etc.

Comic doctors (N.B. All Reade's medical men are comic, and most of them empirics): Drs. Sampson,

Wycherly, Aberford, the leech in *The Cloister and the Hearth*, etc.

Villains (in whom it is impossible to be interested): Mr. Hardie, Noah Skinner, Mr. Meadowes, Peter Crawley, Hawes, Ghysbrecht, etc., and so *ad infinitum*.

We may be certain that whenever a member of our first list comes on the scene, particularly if he is set to anything in the nature of love-making, he will deliver himself in rounded periods — preferably in Latin. The trail of the serpent of prudery and pedantry is over them all.

Take an example: —

Alfred Hardie has been separated from his Julia for a long and agonizing period. It is night; stars twinkle, zephyrs whisper; the bereaved heroine, gazing from her lattice, hears a sigh. Enter the enamoured Alfred with the following amazing speech: —

"Cicero says, *Æquitas ipsa lucet per se*. And yet I hesitate and doubt in a matter of right and wrong like an academic philosopher, weighing and balancing mere academic straws."

Perhaps it is unconsciously done, but certainly Reade is a genius in the particular of placing his good young men in the undignified position of being wooed by women whom they do not love. It requires a St. Antony to retain his equilibrium and avoid looking ridiculous under such circumstances. This fact Reade evidently overlooks, for in every case (those of Alfred and Mrs. Archbold, and Gerard and the Princess Clalia, for instance) he enlarges on the subject with repulsive circumstantiality and detail. In fact, throughout the three books we are more particularly considering, — *Hard Cash*, *It is Never Too Late to Mend*, and *Foul Play*, — our author shows an overwhelming desire to revel in unpleasing particulars. It would have been an immense help to him, as a *genre* writer, if anybody could have brought home to him the truth, that in books, as in civilized life, the operations of the scullery and dressing-room are not considered suitable for exhibition in cultured society.

It is strange that he should have suffered from this tendency, for he lived and wrote before the days when nastiness and physiological monstrosities were considered to give realism to fiction.

It is not so much coarseness in him, as a certain constant tendency to vulgarity in small details; the male side of the quality whose female counterpart produces *Keynotes*, *The Heavenly Twins*, *Salome*, and *Trilby*.

Now, to take the other side of the question, Dickens's characters, although many of them seem to be copies of one another, are specialized, living, breathing entities; complex souls in recognizable, individual bodies. His young men are alive with all the virtues and vices, hopes and little ambitions, tricks of costume and manner, eccentricities and follies, of all the young men any of us know. They act in the vacillating, provisional way in which young men have a habit of acting; and they make their history, instead of merely illustrating a ready-made one. Whether we like or dislike them, we have an interest in them, and are sorry when no more is to be heard of them.

Compare Nicholas Nickleby, David Copperfield, Pip, Herbert Pocket, Martin Chuzzlewit, or Arthur Clennam, with any of Reade's monstrosities, and the reason of the latter's failure to enlist our sympathies will be at once apparent.

Dickens's world is evidently studied from this one in which we suffer and enjoy, only its general trend is visibly upward. His atmosphere is a little purer than this of ours, but we feel we are at home; his very streets and rooms are well known to us, and the faces of his motley company are those of familiar friends. He plays gently and harmoniously on those cords which are common to the fastidious æsthete and the half-civilized squatter. Can any one forget the quiet beauty of Bret Harte's "Dickens in Camp"? The evident truth of this slight poem is a triumphant answer to the accusation sometimes heard that Dickens is too local and too limited in range to attain immortality. Association with his characters is like living with a chatty, good-humored, high-principled companion, in whose society we grow unconsciously better and wiser, whilst forgetting our sins and sorrows, our unpaid bills, and our depression when a pessimistic mood assails us.

We have said that the second requisite of a really good novel should be truth. It seems a paradox, and yet it is not so.

We know perfectly well that theatre scenes are painted canvas, and that the hero's wounds and the heroine's tears are merely shams; but as soon as some hitch in the machinery or ill-directed light forces the fact upon our notice, we lose interest. Our minds never were deceived; but we allowed our senses to be hoodwinked, and have a right to be indignant when our complacency is abused. Reade lets the unreality of his scenes and stories peep through continually; now it is the unearthly virtues of his good people, now the unrelieved badness of his sinners, now one inaccurate technicality, and now another. His design in most of his novels is to expose and correct some crying social abuse, and he does his fighting with a great Teutonic sledge-hammer.

The thuds of a sledge-hammer are not true fiction. We become irritated by the chorus of "Bump! Bump! Bump!" all through the story. We feel like men lost in a maze, in which every path leads up to the same unpleasant bugbear. And if ever we do lose ourselves for a moment in the narrative, out steps the author to nudge us, or supply copious explanations anent the galvanic gambollings of his marionettes.

It is not in human nature to bear these nudgings patiently. Why are we supposed to require the services of the "Flapper" described in *Gulliver's Travels?* Other authors can trust us to digest their good things without having them peptonized for us; and if they suspect their work is above our capacity, they know better than to destroy the verisimilitude of their stories by coming out before the footlights to puff their performances. This unfortunate predilection becomes more marked when Reade undertakes to be funny.

The account of Mrs. Dodd's suitors in chapter thirty-nine of *Hard Cash*, and the overloaded description of how Mr. Hardie cooked his accounts in chapter sixteen, are good examples of this.

In passing we may remark that Reade's humor is not of a high order, being for the most part of a very commonplace burlesque type.

He has comic passages, it is true, such as the death-bed scene of Jane Hardie; but these flashes of fun are not produced intentionally, and owe their piquancy principally to their delightful incongruity.

Judging from this author's singular choice of epithets, one would say that — to adapt Lowell's criticism of Shakespeare — "The hot conception of the author had no time to cool while he was debating the comparative respectability of this word or that; but he snatched what word his instinct prompted;" and in Reade's case his instincts, not being perfectly true, have prompted him wrongly.

Gentlemen and ladies "purr" to each other in his pages; the heroine "gurgles" her love; an "iron young woman" is engaged to nurse an invalid; the second walking-gentlemen's "lion eyes" are continually staring the "dove-like" ones of the second heroine "out of countenance and into love;" and so on and so on, through a whole host of twisted metaphors, grammatical errors, and errors in taste.

He has missed the intimate connection there is between the word and the thing, and has written pages of slipshod English, of which a schoolboy might well be ashamed.

Now Dickens, although verbose and garrulous as befits a writer of his peculiar calibre, is always picturesque and felicitous. He is quite as heated in the warfare of right against wrong as Reade; but he knows that the novel which is only a series of furious diatribes fails of its legitimate aim, and also misses its ostensible one by over-strenuousness.

He knows also that the keen shaft of satire will open joints in armor which will not yield to hammering, and he makes good use of his knowledge. He never calls your attention to the unreality of his puppet-show, not he; he believes in it all himself, and is sure his readers will believe too. His account of things compared to Reade's is as Carlyle's *History of the French Revolution* compared to that of Thiers.

Reade's club, bristling with facts and statistics, is powerless when pitted against Dickens's stiletto.

As regards the third demand we make of a novel, we will not go so far as to say that Reade does not write in an improving manner.

He does elevate the banners of purity, truth, and love — and then blinds us by flapping them in our faces. He advocates district-visiting; but in two of his books he tells us what a thankless office it is, and how little sympathy the objects of our charity have for any woes but their own. (This, by-the-by, proves how little he knows about it. The poor are not unsympathetic, and not more ungrateful than the rich.) Perhaps the fact that the fair district-visitors used their charities unblushingly as a patent balm for heartbreak may explain the unsatisfactory results of their philanthropy.

He makes goodness generally, save in the case of Gerard and Christie Johnstone, a spiritless, colorless thing. We feel, with Mark Twain, that moral excellence is petrifaction, and religious sensibility a disease; and "we don't want to be like any of his good people, we prefer a little healthy wickedness."

Dickens, on the other hand, without arousing our combativeness by preaching, shows us the folly and ridiculousness of being wicked, and leaves color and motion in his good people, so that we can follow in their steps without fear of unwholesome consequences. A comparison of Agnes Wickfield with Jane Hardie or Margaret Brandt will best illustrate our meaning.

It only remains for us to say that, in the matter of

plot and descriptions of stirring incidents by flood and field, Reade as far transcends Dickens as the latter does Reade in other essentials. The works of both authors have acquired through lapse of years that aloofness which allows their relative values to be correctly estimated.

They have gained what in pictures is termed atmosphere. New men, new books, new schemes, are often beautified by a strange charm which disappears with their novelty, and which yet, whilst it prevails, forbids all real criticism of their work. The books of Reade and Dickens have outlived their youthful charm. The special abuses against which they appealed are for the most part abolished.

It remains to be seen how long the man of plot and action will hold his ground against the man of domestic detail and microscopic analysis. The one is essentially the mouthpiece of his place and time, the other the voice of all time and all places.

One of Reade's books, *The Cloister and the Hearth*, has the vital spark in it and will live; the others will not. As for Dickens's works, it may be said of them, as was said of a much greater book, that if his novels were all burnt to-morrow, they could be collected and reconstructed from the hearts of readers, in courts and cottages at home and abroad.

ELLEN CUMPSTON.

ESSAYS

CLARA MIDDLETON

CLARA MIDDLETON

MEREDITH is the Browning of the novel, and whatever may be the popular estimate of his work, to the student it is unique in that it requires something of the concentrative energy that we give to science, if not also a special mental fitness, before it can be thoroughly enjoyed. Hence, those for whom the novel is merely a pastime for an idle hour must leave him to find their recreation in more commonplace fiction. And this preference will not be an indication of the incomprehensibility of Meredith solely, but an evidence of the wrong impression which exists as to the function of classical fiction, and, in regard to Meredith, the quality and nature of his work. *The Egoist*, for example, is comedy — with the Greek flavor; and this qualifying phrase is distinctive, without depreciating either the humor or satire of other novelists.

Hence, in *The Egoist* we may find fresh stimulus for our literary studies, and Clara Middleton may fitly be selected from the mass to show in some points the special method of Meredith in characterization.

It may, indeed, be held that some responsibility is

incurred in making our choice, and that the delicate tints of light and shade in this character, so pleasing to the individual sense in the seclusion of the study, will be destroyed by the inrush of the garish light of publicity. The difficulty of attempting to reconstruct the character by means of criticism (always a clumsy method, but unfortunately the best we know) is fully appreciated; and the attempt to materialize her by projecting her into the world, as seen through the medium of any sense save that of the author's, may seem the grossest sacrilege. Yet the character is so fine a study in the feminine, and affords so many splendid opportunities for contrast and comparison with the feminine creations of other authors, and at the same time gives the further opportunity of saying something about the influences which have gone to mould the characterization of women in English fiction *in the past*, that scruples may be laid to one side for the nonce, and — though at the risk of the charge of egotism — we may proceed to analyze the character.

I say "in the past," because Clara Middleton is a point of departure from the conventional characterization of women in English fiction. The moral forces which have dominated and restrained the artist's hand hitherto are here wholly set aside; but a master-hand has effected the changes, and they are wrought so strongly and withal so delicately, that the character has passed the usual criticism without attracting the notice that it would have attracted had they been wrought by one less skilful at his craft.

There are two points in the character to which we may give special attention, as their combination has hitherto been considered impracticable, if we look at them from the point of view of the traditional character with which the older novelists of the nineteenth century have invested women in English fiction.

In the first place, Clara Middleton is essentially English. This, it may be presumed, the majority of readers feel instinctively, and believe because of the affirmation of instinct, rather than because it may be shown by a critical estimate of the character. It is necessary, however, to make this estimate; for the other characteristic which Meredith has developed in Clara Middleton would not have been such a singular innovation had it not been combined with one that is peculiarly English.

Let us, then, begin by saying that she has that sobriety of mind and temperament which is a truly national characteristic, and which is the product of our insularity and our social morality. Some insistence might be given to this point; because we can no more mould or approximate to the English character upon any Continental model than we can fly, and this even in despite of our modern cosmopolitan culture. Our national character has a peculiar flavor — if I may so phrase it — in this respect, and it is impossible to define it with any great exactitude; but it is so truly the outgrowth of our institutions and training that none but the wilfully blind can mistake the phlegm or stoicism of some of our Continental neighbors for this English sobriety, which combines at once serene self-possession with enterprise and effort for precedence.

Then we have, in addition to this, that love of liberty and nature which is our common heritage,—the love of liberty common to all the English, and of nature according to the opportunities which are held out by the circumstances and conditions of our lives. For it may be said with perfect truth that the instinctive love of nature is as truly a characteristic of the English as the love of liberty; but it is suppressed in many instances by the more serious business of life.

In the character of Clara Middleton, Meredith has blended each with admirable precision. The limitations of Sir Willoughby Patterne's domains are in her mind always associated with the narrow, prescribed area of his mind; and she is painfully aware that the scope for her activities in the future when she has become his wife are too circumscribed for her nature. The great point insisted upon here by the novelist is the perfect poise which her love of nature and liberty gives to her deportment; and this adjustment to which her life conforms, and by which it is governed, is the ideal characteristic of the English.

Then add to this her variety — her whims and fancies, if you choose, or, as her father calls them, "the prerogative of the feminine." Is there not here a reflex of the climate, with its alternations of cloud and shine, of tempest and peace? All this appears to me so essentially English, that I must apologize for treating of it here. I am afraid, after all, that the instinctive feeling that she *is* English will outweigh any calm analysis that pretended to separate the different elements, and show that the ultimate result of the combination is to make the Englishwoman. But, as I said before, it is to make the comparison between this characteristic and another that is essentially un-English that I do it.

Then, what is this un-English and antagonistic element in Clara Middleton which makes her so essentially unlike the traditional heroine of the English novel? I would define it simply as sensuousness. She is not only beautiful, but sensuously beautiful; and in order to emphasize the definition, let me call to my aid an illustration, symbolical and subtle, because natural, — the Greek myth of Venus — the goddess rising from the bath in all her sensuous beauty, and striking the luckless hunter blind. This, it appears to me, if we eliminate the anger of the goddess as a conventional interpolation of a later age, is the universal symbol of love which strikes with blindness all who are unfortunately affected. And it applies to Clara Middleton, — though on the surface there does not seem to be any singularity in this, for it may be said that all the novelists have unconsciously echoed the symbolism of the Greek. Its application to the character under discussion lies in this, that while she dazzles all beholders with her charms, she also exercises to the full that mysterious sexual power which is and has ever been the prerogative of the woman.

But here let me remark, lest I should misinterpret Meredith, and unduly shock those who uphold the traditional method of the English novelists, that the sensuousness of Clara Middleton, though analogous to that element which we meet with in everyday life, is not of the common quality. There is visible in Meredith's creation neither moral laxity nor the mental aberration which constitutes the danger of the characteristic. It is ideal, subordinated, and subservient to the highest art. There is nothing that the prurient may revel in or the moralists cavil at; but it is impossible to help ourselves from gliding into the atmosphere of sensuousness wherein Meredith has enveloped his creation. Sir Willoughby Patterne feels the charm acutely, after she has wounded his egoism:—

"He placed an exceedingly handsome and flattering young widow of his acquaintance . . . beside Clara for a comparison; involuntarily, and at once . . . in despite of Lady Mary's high birth and connections as well, the silver lustre of the maid sicklied the poor widow."

And Vernon Whitford's experience is also telling:—

"Take your chin off your hand, your elbow off your book, and fix yourself," said Vernon, wrestling with the seduction of Crossjoy's idolatry; for Miss Middleton's appearance had been preternaturally sweet on her departure, and the next pleasure to seeing her was hearing of her from the lips of this passionate young poet."

The Doctor's babbling in "the aged and great wine" scene is also effective: —

"I hoped once . . . but she is a girl. The nymph of the woods is in her. Still she will bring you her flower-cup of Hippocrene. She has that aristocracy — the noblest. She is fair. . . . She has no history. You are the first heading of the chapter. With you she will have one tale, as it should be. You know — most fragrant she that smells of nought — she goes to you from me, from me alone, from her father to her husband."

And then follows the experience of Sir Willoughby as he had seen her: —

"Distressingly sweet; . . . sweet with sharpness of young sap. Her eyes, her lips, her fluttering dress that played happy mother across her bosom; and her laughter, her slim figure, peerless carriage, all her terrible sweetness touched his wound to the smarting quick."

And her sensuous influence even affects the boy Crossjoy.

"Miss Middleton lay back on the grass, and said, 'Are you going to be fond of me, Crossjoy?'

"The boy sat blinking. His desire was to prove that he was immoderately fond of her already, and he might have flown at her neck had she been sitting up, but her recumbancy and eyelids half-closed excited wonder in him and awe. His young heart beat fast."

These examples are sufficient for the purpose of showing Meredith's sensuous envelopment of the character. And it is simply a confirmation of our experience, that he, by combining these characteristics, has been truer in his delineations than those which have been before him in English fiction. For we all know, and it is tacitly acknowledged, that the sensuous charm of the feminine is at all times operative. But it is a fact that the older novelists have omitted or disguised with one consent; as if it were possible, in analyzing the motives of marriage, or the physiology of love, to leave the sexual passion out of consideration.

Take Thackeray as an example. His good women are nearly always insipid, —

> "Too good
> For human nature's daily food."

In *Pendennis*, Laura Bell is the representative of the coming woman; she is quite English, too, and hence, I think, may be fitly chosen for comparison with Clara Middleton. In what, then, does she differ from Meredith's heroine? Simply in this, — that Thackeray has hidden from view the most womanly side of the feminine nature; she is full of incomparable excellences, but, as woman, she is wofully incomplete as a study in human nature, and beside the creation of Meredith, she pales with ineffectual fires. Thackeray gives us the unfinished sketch; Meredith has filled in the shading.

And Thackeray is not alone in his incompleteness of the study of the feminine; generally speaking, our novelists have not dared to deal with the hidden emotions of life, or, if they have, they have dealt with them impalpably, and glozed them over with a cloud of verbiage, and left their meanings to the imagination.

Dickens's studies in this respect are inconceivably ridiculous. He can paint the superficial emotions, and exaggerate pathos; but he makes you weep for joy when he attempts to reconcile his art in the delineation of the female character with the conventional moral prejudice of the English people. Take an example from *Dombey and Son:* he makes Dombey's wife leave her husband and go off to the Continent with Carker. At the conclusion of the journey, poor Carker gets, instead of loving caresses, the promise of a knife, and the reader gets a melodrama. It is an elopement badly conceived and worse executed. One is tempted to ask what good reasons had Dickens for covering this woman with shame, — for he arouses the worst of our social prejudices when he makes her elope with Carker, — and then refrain from giving us the inevitable result of the elopement. It is hardly possible to imagine anything more foreign to human nature than Dickens's conception; it is false to experience, and yet more false to art.

And Charlotte Brontë's *Jane Eyre* is hardly better in execution. There are any number of excellent reasons to justify Rochester's treatment of Jane Eyre, but no amount of reason would have justified him had the marriage ceremony been performed. The catastrophe which takes place on the morning of the wedding just averts our prejudice, and saves the reputation of the novelist. Here, too, you will see, our moral censorship has to be appeased, and character and circumstances have to be moulded to suit our preconceived notions of these things.

Even George Eliot must bow to the inevitable. The novelist may mould her life on a principle above the criticism of society, but these instincts must not appear in her conception of feminine nature in her books. Maggie Tulliver, in the *Mill on the Floss*, must die an unnatural death, — is drowned to appease the savage instincts of our conventional morality. And every one must have been struck with the immense difference which exists between Shakespeare's conception of the passionate Italian nature in *Romeo and Juliet*, and George Eliot's conception of the same passionate Italian nature in *Romola*. Shakespeare, of course, was not influenced by these conventional restraints, and could afford to be true to humanity and art; but George Eliot could not, and hence Romola is Italian only when seen through the English spectacles of George Eliot, and the passionate Italian nature is subdued by the cold and bloodless morality of the English people in the nineteenth century.

Hence, then, Meredith appears to me to be the point of departure, as I said at the outset, for the better treatment of the feminine in the future.

But I would not stop here; if Meredith has betrayed one of the fundamental canons of the English novelist's craft, he has also effected a reconciliation between it and art.

In Clara Middleton we approach nearer to Shakespeare's conception of woman's nature and purpose, with its natural artistic setting in frame of gold. She is an artistic triumph, both in conception and achievement; "true to the kindred points of heaven and home."

Becky Sharp, which I take to be one of the greatest achievements in English fiction — in the feminine — judged purely from the standpoint of art, is incomplete when compared with Meredith's heroine; there are unimagined details in her life which Thackeray omitted; periods when Becky drops out of existence, and even the denizens of *Vanity Fair* could take no cognizance of her actions. Now, this is due to one of two reasons: either it is due to the instinctive sense of proportion in the artist, or it is due to the influence which the current morality exercised over him in this particular direction, with the rest of his brethren, making him subordinate his art to conventional moral prejudice.

This last I take to be the true reason, and in chapter sixty-four in *Vanity Fair* he says so himself.

Here, then, is the artist's acknowledgment of his failure to complete his ideal, owing to certain predominant notions of morality prevailing in his auditory. He must mix his colors in lives in accordance with the preferential tastes of society. He may, and he *has*, drawn in lines that are indeed most strongly suggestive. This is forgiven, so long as the naked reality is hidden; but the picture is still incomplete, and all these gaps and evasions noticeable in Becky's career mar the perfection of his work, and rasp upon our nerves, making us wish that the rigidly moral tone of English social life had not been so strongly developed as to come perennially into collision with the artist's conception, and make ideal achievement impossible.

And Meredith, while giving in the characterization of Clara Middleton an artistic completeness, has left nothing to cavil at in the sensuous charm which he has thrown around her.

I am aware that there is a stage, as where wit degenerates into buffoonery, so where artistic license in limning the erotic emotions degenerates into licentiousness. But the days of Wycherley and Congreve, with their exaggerated emphasis on the vices of society, are over in English literature. Theirs was not art; it was the portrayal of sensuality and vicious pleasure for its own sake. And the delineation of vice which arises from the morbid pleasure of steeping the poetic faculty in sensual desire is perhaps after all the worst prostitution of the artist's power.

Meredith avoids everything in our human instincts which would tend to debase his ideal. He deals with the hidden emotions of life only to lift them out of the commonplace, and set them where, with true poetic insight, he sees they will appear, not to the untutored imagination, but to minds fitted to receive the subtle intuitions of a master. And he has withal the power to evoke the soft and radiant light which has ever been the strongest bond between master and disciple, and which is a truer guide to the master's thought than any skilled criticism which does not vibrate this sympathetic medium.

Clara Middleton is comparable to an English spring morning, with its inexpressible charm, when the earth is blushing with life, and the sun is veiling his face like a coy maiden with the thin gray mist that rises over wood and field; when the air is instinct, and the birds are singing their sweetest song of praise in honor of the new-born day.

This is the time when nature appeals most directly to us, by unveiling the sensuous, glowing side of creation, and the ordinary processes of life are glorified by the divine instinct which is flowing through our veins, and tingling into pleasant sensitiveness the dormant chords of our lives. Whoever has been penetrated with these emotions of nature in the spring days, when "Nature is tremulous with excess of joy," has felt the charm which rises from the contemplation of the rich and rare embodiment of feminine qualities in Clara Middleton.

JOSEPH FAIRNEY.

ESSAYS

THE IDEAL OF ASCETICISM

THE IDEAL OF ASCETICISM

The Cloister and the Hearth is a book of considerable power and ability, which its author has come very near to spoiling, from the æsthetic point of view, by a most unhappy sentence, and an irritating foot-note thereto attached. The sentence is on the last page but one, and is as follows:—

"I ask your sympathy, then, for their rare constancy and pure affection, and their cruel separation by a vile heresy in the bosom of the Church; but not your pity for their early but happy end."

The foot-note attached to "vile heresy" is "Celibacy of the clergy, an invention truly fiendish." The writer of this essay would beg leave to urge that this sentence and its foot-note are to be reprobated, whatever views we may hold on the particular subject mentioned, because they unveil in a crude and inartistic manner a purpose which the story itself, told as it is with such power and pathos, would leave sufficiently prominent, and because they deal in far too summary a fashion with a tangled and difficult subject. The ascetic idea is a many-sided one, taking varying forms under varying circumstances. And it should be observed at the outset that it is not by any means the invention of Catholic Christianity, although in our minds it is very largely associated with it. It is by an examination of the principles on which asceticism has based itself, and of the varying forms in which it has been exhibited, that we may hope to get some view of our subject, — "the ideal of asceticism."

There was a great deal of asceticism of a monastic type deeply interwoven in the old religions of the East, such as Buddhism, and the religion of the Persian Zoroaster. Indeed, monasticism constitutes the central feature of the former. It seems to have exhibited itself in the shape of a desire to retire from the impediments of ordinary life, and to seek after a philosophic calm and contemplation, together with an emancipation as complete as possible from the enchaining passions and affections of the flesh. It was a stage to which every true Buddhist was expected to attain sooner or later in his religious life. Such an asceticism was inseparably connected with a principle common to all the prominent systems of philosophy and religion in the East — a belief in the inherent evil of things material, and so of the flesh and the natural affections. This type of asceticism was a marked feature in the philosophy of the Greek Pythagoras; and it appears strongly, though in a modified form, in the writings of Plato and Aristotle. It is modified by the very great stress laid by these and by most Greek thinkers on a man's duty as a citizen.

Christianity, then, found already existing in the natures of its Oriental converts a very strong tendency towards monasticism; and the circumstances by which early Christianity was surrounded, and the unswerving standard of high morality which Christianity upheld, alike contributed to foster it. For Christian monasticism sprang into being as a revolt from the frightful wickedness which accompanied the decay of Pagan civilization. The hideous license existing in the Roman empire in the days of early Christianity has been painted in lurid colors by many writers, and the church did not hesitate to make a strong practical protest against it. To the Christian the imperative call seemed to be to come out from the midst of a world of hopeless depravity. It can hardly be considered a matter of wonder that early Christian asceticism soon ran into excessive and exaggerated forms.

It was in Egypt that monasticism took deepest root, and in the third and fourth centuries there were many thousands of monks living in the desert retreats of that country. Egyptian monasticism took a most exaggerated form. An absurd and disproportionate stress was laid upon certain portions of the gospel teaching. Passages such as, "He that loveth father or mother more than me is not worthy of me," were distorted beyond all recognition, until it became a virtue to desert even Christian parents in the most relentlessly cruel manner. Many stories are to be found in Lecky's *History of European Morals* illustrative of this. Mortification of the flesh was pursued to the most rigorous extreme, and the body was lacerated and starved in the fierce endeavor to eradicate every vestige of the natural appetites of mankind. Many of the Egyptian monks lived in solitude, wrestling in utter loneliness with the powers of evil which seemed to infect the whole world. The effect of such a life of austerity and solitude was often simply to foster the horrible visions and imaginations of evil from which the monk sought to rid himself. The true proportion of morality was thrown out, and the domestic virtues were rigorously suppressed. "To break by his ingratitude the heart of the mother who had borne him, to persuade the wife who adored him that it was her duty to separate from him forever, to abandon his children, uncared for and beggars, to the mercies of the world, was regarded by the true hermit as the most acceptable offering he could make to his God. His business was to save his own soul."

The great St. Jerome, who did much to foster and encourage monasticism, endeavored to regulate these austerities and to restrain the more exaggerated forms of mortification; and as time went on, this excess was gradually regulated. But it was with the growth of that type of monasticism which St. Benedict founded, that a better order of things came about. The earlier

THE IDEAL OF ASCETICISM. 79

monasticism in its fanatical devotion could think of nothing but the suppression of all that was earthly; and even learning of all kinds was rigorously avoided, and no useful work of any sort was undertaken. The Benedictine monasteries, on the other hand, were centres of civilization and industry, doing much for the pursuit of learning, and tilling the soil of Italy. In fact, the strong practical bent of the Roman mind produced a type of asceticism essentially different to that of the mystic Oriental and the philosophic Greek. It was an asceticism with a purpose, instead of an asceticism which sought its end in the suppression of all that was human. Dean Milman, the author of the *History of Latin Christianity*, is no lover of monasticism in any form, but he gives its due praise to the best Western monasticism. "Western monasticism," he says, "in its general character, was not the barren, idly laborious, or dreamy quietude of the East. It was industrious and productive: it settled colonies, preserved arts and letters, built splendid edifices, fertilized deserts. If it rent from the world the most powerful minds, having trained them by its stern discipline, it sent them back to rule the world. It continually, as it were, renewed its youth, and kept up a constant infusion of vigorous life; now quickening into enthusiasm, now darkening into fanaticism, and by its perpetual rivalry stimulating the zeal or supplying the deficiencies of the secular clergy. In successive ages it adapted itself to the state of the human mind. At first a missionary to barbarous nations, it built abbeys, hewed down forests, cultivated swamps, enclosed domains, retrieved or won for civilization tracts which had fallen into waste or had never known culture. With St. Dominic it turned its missionary zeal upon Christianity itself, and spread as a preaching order throughout Christendom; with St. Francis it became even more popular, and lowered itself to the very humblest of mankind." And again he speaks of Western monasticism "as the missionary of what was holy and Christian in the new civilization; as the chief maintainer, if not the restorer, of agriculture in Italy; as the cultivator of the forests and morasses of the north; as the apostle of the heathen who dwelt beyond the pale of the Western empire."

In a word, it was characteristic of Eastern monasticism to content itself with the morbid desire to repress the affections and to save the soul of the individual monk; it was characteristic of the Western asceticism that it associated men together, schooled them, and disciplined them by a life of regulated self-denial, so as to make them available for high and useful purposes.

This very rough and inadequate survey of different types of asceticism has been made with the purpose of leading up to principles; and it should be borne in mind that, in all that has been said, only general tendencies have been indicated, and the description of monasticism in these different forms is only true in the broad.

The principle I would now wish to state is this: asceticism is true or false, good or bad, according as it is what may be called athletic (following a well-known metaphor of St. Paul), or dualistic. This needs explanation. And first, what is dualism? Dualism is a system of thought which builds itself on the eternal antagonism of two principles, one good and the other bad. Its most obvious form is that which pervades Oriental philosophies and religions. It teaches that matter is inherently and essentially bad. Only spirit can be inherently and essentially good. The body, or the flesh, is hopelessly and unquestionably bad; the soul, in so far as it can be freed from the flesh, is good. The object and aim of existence is, therefore, to crush and ill-use the body, and restrain as far as possible every bodily want and appetite, however innocent. This system of thought existed in Persia and India centuries before the appearance of Christianity. It is sometimes known as "Manichæism," because in Christian times a Persian heretic named Manes developed it, and endeavored, with partial success, to infect Christianity with it. It is to be observed that Manichæism does not teach simply that the flesh is evil when over-indulged, or that such and such an act is evil if carried to excess, but that the act is under all circumstances hopelessly wrong. Marriage, to the Oriental dualist, is as wrong as what is generally recognized as immorality. Eating and drinking are only to be just tolerated because suicide is wrong, and a man is bound to keep himself alive. This kind of thought is ever reappearing, and the moralist has ever to be on his watch against it. It is to be found in the Puritanism which forbids *absolutely* certain pleasures, such as music and dancing, innocent in themselves, and only wrong when carried to excess, or prostituted to low uses. An illustration of it is to be found even now among a certain class of temperance advocates, who hold that to touch a drop of intoxicating liquor is under all circumstances sinful. Such a system of thought is pernicious, not only because it is in itself false, but because in history it has always been known to produce violent reactions into the opposite extremes of vice and license. It is a demon which has been exorcised over and over again, but which is ever reappearing. Now, it is the asceticism which founds itself on principles such as these, which is bad. It makes a vain attempt to eradicate natural appetites and affections which are given to mankind for a certain purpose, and are only bad when uncontrolled and indulged under unlawful circumstances. Christians who are misled into an asceticism of this type are false to their own principles; for they forget that the God whom they serve created the body

THE IDEAL OF ASCETICISM.

as well as the soul, and that the Son of God has dignified the body by living an incarnate life. It was only the extreme wickedness and degradation that resulted from the decay of a great civilization which made such an asceticism possible in the Christian church. Certain numbers of early Christians, flying in horror from the revolting immorality of the world about them, ran into this opposite extreme. A better type of monasticism did, as has been shown, grow up; but monasticism has hardly ever been wholly free from this Manichæan taint.

It is characteristic, also, of a monasticism thus tainted, that it holds strange and false theories as to the meritoriousness of acts of self-denial and mortification. Such acts come to be regarded, not merely as part of a discipline intended to school the individual for certain noble ends, but as in themselves meritorious. So much mortification will buy off so much purgatory hereafter. A certain amount of needless pain suffered on earth acquires thus a commercial value, and represents so much purchasing power for pleasure in heaven.

The asceticism based on a good principle I have called athletic, and for this reason. Asceticism is a word derived from the Greek word, ἄσκησις (askesis), which means "training," or "practice," and generally athletic training. So athletic asceticism is, in fact, an asceticism which is true to its name. It treats the body, not as something inherently evil, but as an instrument, a useful servant given for high purposes; but to be carefully kept in order lest it become the master; to be kept in good trim for its master's use. . "I keep under my body and bring it into subjection," says St. Paul; or, more literally, "I buffet my body and lead it about as a slave." According to this principle, the body is to be disciplined, not crushed; the whole man is to be developed; nothing is in itself to be called common or unclean. The bad asceticism tried vainly to crush the bodily affections, family ties, and the intellect. The good asceticism seeks to control by inflexible but rational laws the bodily affections, to sanctify family ties, and to consecrate the intellect to the highest possible pursuits. It is difficult to imagine a character more opposed to the bad asceticism than that of Gerard in *The Cloister and the Hearth*. His nature is all aglow with family affections of a noble type, as seen in his love for his parents, and in his pure passion for Margaret. His artistic sensibilities are keen and highly trained; and he is drawn to the church, not only by his deep piety, but by his strong scholarly instincts, which make him such a delightful character to study. The course of reckless vice through which he went in Rome, and the opposite extreme of fantastic asceticism by which he tried to master himself in the cave at Gouda, were but episodes, bad dreams, brought about by strong revulsions of feeling which temporarily overmastered him.

There is a good deal of hard hitting at monks and their ways in the book; but it should be remembered that the monastic system is shown in its pages to produce its attractive as well as its hard and relentless characters — its Anselm as well as its Jerome; and it did much in a dark and turbulent age for the protection and propagation of learning and scholarship, without which Gerard and Magnus Erasmus could never have lived before us, the one in fiction, and the other in history.

But the object of the book is, of course, to write down the celibacy of the clergy. We should know that well enough without that infelicitous sentence and dreadful foot-note before alluded to; but we must return to them for a moment to see how our subject of the ascetic ideal is affected by the question of the celibacy of the clergy. Charles Reade states his case in too summary and hasty a fashion. He forgets that there were sound and rational motives at work, as well as unsound and mistaken ones, among those who brought about the enforced celibacy of the clergy in the Latin Church. There is a distinct call for celibate clergy, for certain purposes. In certain spheres of the church's work, especially in missionary work, and in some parts of large cities, the work of celibate priests will be obviously more effective, more free and unhampered, than that of married clergy, with the impediments of a wife and family. A man who takes up this class of work must be like a soldier equipped for active service, and he will be missing his vocation if he does anything to make himself a less effective instrument for the work. He is called to greater self-denial than other men. But any system which teaches that marriage is essentially a lower state than celibacy, and therefore requires that those who are employed for sacred functions must not so far degrade themselves as to marry, is but involved once again in the oft-exorcised dualism, and is confounding things wrong in themselves with things wrong only under certain circumstances. Such teaching is tainted with the old poison of Manichæism over again, which takes a low view of marriage, making it only less bad than direct immorality.

No asceticism is true which does not contemplate the development of the whole man in the best and fullest sense. It will not trample what is merely earthly, but it recognizes the need of discipline in the interests of something higher. The lower nature is to be kept rigorously under control; to be denied and repressed when its assertion conflicts with the higher, and demands a satisfaction which circumstances make unlawful. For, after all, asceticism is but the proper recognition of a higher element than that which is merely animal; and therefore will not allow an unregulated or excessive pursuit of any pleasure, however innocent it may be in itself. It is the call to sacrifice. Robert Browning has some noble, but characteristically awkward expressions on the subject in *Rabbi Ben Ezra:*—

> " Poor vaunt of life indeed
> Were man but formed to feed
> On joy, to solely seek and find and feast;
> Such feasting ended, then
> As sure an end to men;
> Irks care the crop-full bird ?   Frets doubt the
>   maw-crammed beast ?
>
> .   .   .   .
>
> Then welcome each rebuff
> That turns earth's smoothness rough,
> Each sting that bids, nor sit, nor stand, but go!
> Be our joy three-parts pain!
> Strive, and hold cheap the strain;
> Learn, nor account the pang; dare, never grudge
>   the throe."

To sum up — the ideal asceticism is not a useless mortification pursued for its own ends, but a discipline with a purpose in view. The ascetic may, in certain circumstances, be called to give up certain family ties; but he will not consider that the isolated act is in itself meritorious, and he will not underrate or take a low view of family ties for others; while recognizing the temptations of the flesh when undisciplined, he will not insult his body by needless or purposeless severities. A young Northumbrian poet has stated the case well. To a Northumbrian audience it will be of interest to state his name. It is Lord Warkworth, who has this year carried off the Newdigate prize at Oxford with a poem on St. Francis d'Assisi, distinctly above the ordinary level of prize compositions. Dealing with the well-known story of St. Francis's vision of the stigmata or marks of Christ's passion, he puts these words into the mouth of the saint: —

— " Then I understood
The vision: 'In my *flesh* should I see God,' —
That flesh which I had deemed the prison-cell
That clogs th' aspiring soul; th' unlovely shell
That hides the young life of the tender grain,
Shall in transfigured beauty robe again
The ripened ears of harvest! Strange it were,
Did pain please God, who made His world so fair!
They serve Him best whose kindled spirits move
In perfect cadence with His life of love."
C. G. HALL.

ESSAYS

CHARACTER DEVELOPMENT IN "ROMOLA"

CHARACTER DEVELOPMENT IN "ROMOLA"

THE great purpose of George Eliot in *Romola* is to show the effect of circumstance upon the development of the human character.

We may first turn aside to note other illustrations of character development. A young man, who has hitherto been the acknowledged pattern of the village, in an evil hour gives way to temptation, and finally becomes more dissolute and dangerous than all his neighbors. This is character *development*, — a character not assumed or acted, but real and cultivated.

Who has not trembled as he has sat within the soul of Lady Macbeth while the terrible storm is accumulating? She has only succeeded in *acting* a character, she has not developed one. She has taken intoxicating drink, and temporarily succeeded in paralyzing her higher self; but that artificial influence has gone, and the old character remains inexorable. Although opportunity has inflamed a long smouldering ambition, that ambition has failed to call to its aid any embryonic character germs. The higher must not live, the lower nature will not germinate; and that which happens is just what must happen under the circumstances. Reason resigns her seat in the conflict.

The more we think of the vibrations produced by tempting circumstance upon our own moral natures, the more we realize the truth of George Eliot's philosophy, and the subtlety of her intellect. Silas Marner creeps away from society in general; it seems to him that the world is so incomprehensibly big and mysteriously peopled. Under an altered environment his social and religious proclivities give way to imbecile selfishness. While his character thus hardens into abstract avarice, the living world seems to have no existence for him, except as a mysterious monster that gives him gold for labor. But his gold at length is stolen from him, and now there is nothing for that silent heart to love in silence. For a heart that has the germs of love in it, and fails to find another heart to reciprocate affection, will waste its sweetness upon the inanimate, or it will burst. So it was with Silas. Sally — faithless Sally — first opened her heart to his love, but shut it again; and we find that when Sally is no more to him his affection becomes transfused to love of wealth. But another accident occurs. A little child, whose mother lies dead in the snow, totters into the cottage of Silas just at the moment when life seems most intolerable. And what happens? From that moment poverty becomes bliss. Here at once is a substitute in a living reality for the lost gold. And no hand better than George Eliot's could have shown how wonderfully, yet naturally, the buried germs of a long-dead life bloom forth under the influence of this child, and how Silas tastes the fulness of a great character in his old age.

It is always the story of a soul she tells. We are instantly enveloped in a pyschological atmosphere; for while some writers keep one in the outer world, and give only in lightning flashes furtive glances into the inner life, she takes us there, and there we remain, and thence look out upon the surface of existence. Who has not felt as though he dwelt really within the offended soul of Gwendolen, who married for gold and position, expecting thereby to pacify a soul left celibate? But outward ease did not bring into peace; the lightsome innocence of her character becomes displaced, and dark and hitherto unsuspected thoughts take possession of her whole being, bubbling forth unbidden, as instincts do.

In *Silas Marner*, beautiful and complete in itself as it is, we have only the preface, to which *Romola* is the accomplished fact. While *Silas Marner* is perfect in its simplicity, *Romola* is great in its complexity. We must remember the stupendous historic background of the story — Florence with all her ancient grandeur, her teeming inhabitants with their cries of joy, of pain, of hope, of revenge; and above all is heard the clarion voice of Savonarola rushing through the Florentine soul like a mad river. All this gigantic background is conjured up to show — what? The evolution of one beautiful life!

Great and good people always leave their souls behind them, whether it be in statuary, or books, or deeds. George Eliot has left her living soul with Romola. A statue is left by a master — a statue with a soul in it, that makes us feel when we look upon it as though we were in the presence of an extraordinary being. Its eyes are stone, yet they gaze down into the deep recesses of our being; no affection can be forced upon it, no secret can be hidden from its sight; we dare not touch its garment, nor utter nor think an unholy thought in its presence. As such a statue is Romola introduced to us. Her silence is greater than eloquence, and her coldness comes of holiness. She is rigid, yet as sensitive as the sensitive plant. She is touched by love, — blind love, — and the whole mechanism of a great character is set in motion. She is touched by falsehood, and she seems to return to marble again. Romola's inward beauties are developed in adversity and sorrow. She wrestles with her poorer self; Tito wrestles with his higher self. Tito deals out his soul to evade unpleasant duties, only to find that the unperformed remain everlasting debts that accumulate and increase unhappiness, until finally all pleasure is swallowed up, and life becomes a wide, trackless waste of misery.

There are turning-points in all our lives — there are "currents" that must be taken when they "serve," or the most important opportunity of our life is lost. There is often much that is unpleasant to perform ere we taste a morsel of real happiness. Pleasures often come only from outward satisfaction; happiness can only come from the soul. Happiness once attained owes much of its sweetness to the pain that has been experienced in the struggle to obtain it; for, as it is stated in the proem to *Romola* : —

"Little children are still the symbol of the eternal marriage between love and duty;"

and —

"Life to be highest must be made up of conscious voluntary sacrifice."

Here is Tito at a point where lanes meet and diverge. This way is thorny, but the soul says, "Go;" the other way is apparently pleasant, but it leads to ruin. We find him saying: —

"Can any philosophy prove to me that I was bound to care for another's sufferings more than for my own? . . . The world belongs to youth and strength, and these glories are his who can extract more pleasures out of them. . . . Baldazzar has had his draught of life; . . . it is my turn now."

Thus we find that, when the presiding will of his father sits no longer over him, Tito's character finds its polarity in selfishness, and we have the first and all-important glimmer of Tito in an undreamed-of character.

It is interesting to watch how with wondrous rapidity these newly awakened germs develop, whilst those which lay uppermost in his character as hitherto known just as rapidly drop out of activity. His unconquerable love of self, his horror of unpleasant duties, gradually crush the higher manhood out of him. The communings with the soul become less and less protracted. Desire becomes the master of conscience; and the embodiment of truth which he once reverenced in Romola becomes now the personification of an inexorable Nemesis. Twin sisters are cowardice and selfishness — while selfishness is ever directing the nervous fingers of avarice, cowardice puts in every crevice of thought a skeleton.

Yet Romola is not perfect; she, too, has her antipathy to painful duties. But while he shrinks from duty because of its unpleasantness, and is conscious of the unrighteousness, she turns from duty through ignorance.

Romola has been reared in a world of dead wisdom, yet she has sucked in truth. She knows the book of life only as it has been translated. Tito came to her with his living smiles and his love as a revelation. But truth has gone from him, and she can no longer love him; and loveless cohabitation is to her the lowest depth of degradation. She would fly from falsehood because her soul abhors it, and live a death in life. But the voice of Savonarola arrests her; and, while she fancies that hitherto the deepest reaches of her soul have been self-sounded, she is convinced ere long that that which she accepted as holiness in the abstract was not unsmitten by selfishness.

"What has your dead wisdom done for you, my daughter? It has left you without a heart for the neighbours among whom you dwell. . . . When the sword has pierced your side, you say, I will go away; I cannot bear my sorrow. . . . You would leave your place empty, when it ought to be filled with your pity and your labour. If there is wickedness in the streets, your steps should shine with light and purity; if there is a cry of anguish, you, my daughter, because you know the meaning of it, ought to be there to still it. . . . Sorrow has come to teach you a new religion. . . . My daughter, every bond of life is a debt; the right lies in the payment of that debt — it can lie nowhere else."

And so it does. Is it not in this tendency in human character to fly from the unpleasant, and the bringing of it back again by higher and more powerful influences, that the hidden virtues of characters are often called into permanent activity? Truly, "no man or woman can choose their duties, any more than they can choose their father, or mother, or birthplace."

Thus accident has given Romola another and a truer and wider view of human duties. She had hitherto only known how sweet it was to be holy as defined in keeping one's self apart from that which is unholy. But holiness must now have no root in selfhood. "Father," she says, "I will be guided. Teach me. I will go back." Life, to be rightly lived, must not consist in doing no evil, like a statue in a busy thoroughfare, but in practising a religion that has few words and many deeds. There is no cathedral so beautiful as one white soul; no organ so expressive as one honest voice; and no religion more holy than one good deed. No man exists for himself alone, and a life has not fulfilled its mission unless the happiness of the community is increased by it. There is no abstraction; all are links to one great chain of conscious existence; and if we sever ourselves, our strength is as naught to us, for we gain nothing, and the purpose of our life is then destroyed.

As a stone thrown into a lake causes every drop of water to be affected, so an accidental circumstance may prove the turning-point, not of one, but of many lives. We have seen how Tito's accident became the beginning of a degenerate life — a starting-point to a most beautiful life is furnished in Romola. But in Baldazzer the case is different. There is no development of a sane or embryonic character; intellectual darkness comes over it, relieved now and then with flashes of memory, like lightning in a midnight thunderstorm, making only two projections visible, — remorse and revenge.

We have seen how beneath the magic influence of Savonarola the inward majesty of Romola's character comes out; for during the pestilence, where there is a "cry of anguish," is she not there "to still it"? and where there is wickedness in the streets, do not "her steps shine with light and purity"?

Yet another great change comes over Romola. The voice of Savonarola, which has hitherto swept through her soul like music that is more felt than heard, has now lost its power. She has lost her faith in him; and "with the sinking of human trust the dignity of life sinks too; we cease to believe in our own better self, since that also is part of the common nature which is degraded in our thought; and all finer influences of the soul are dulled." She longed for repose; she was tired of the weary world; she felt "the spring of her once active piety drying up," and again her egoism of self predominated. Her bonds that once bound her to Tito are beyond all power to reunite. "It is too late, Tito," she finally says, "there is no killing the suspicion that deceit has once begotten. . . . I, too, am a human being. I have a soul of my own that abhors your actions. Our union is a pretence—as if a perpetual lie could be a sacred marriage."

Out of every difficulty Tito comes more degraded. His smile becomes slave to his base intrigues, and lines gather and deepen about his mouth. But every sorrow makes Romola more radiant. Her "barren egoistic complainings" drift her, not to selfish repose, but to the very place where a great soul is needed; and the truth of Savonarola's words is beautifully confirmed: —

"The draught is bitter on the lips. But there is a rapture in the cup — there is the vision that makes all life below it dross forever."

THOMAS DAWSON.

The Literary Study of the Bible.

An Account of the Leading Forms of Literature represented in the Sacred Writings. Intended for English Readers. By RICHARD G. MOULTON. University Extension Professor of English Literature in the University of Chicago; late Extension Lecturer in Literature to Cambridge University (England), and to the London and the American Societies for the Extension of University Teaching. Author of "Shakespeare as a Dramatic Artist," "The Ancient Classical Drama," etc. Cloth. ooo pages. Retail price, $0.00.

THIS work is founded on the experience of University Extension Courses delivered during three years in various parts of England and America, in connection with universities or with churches of all denominations.

It deals with the Bible as literature, without reference to theological or distinctively religious matters on the one hand, or on the other hand to the historical analysis which has come to be known as "the higher criticism." With a view to the general reader it endeavors to bring out the literary interest of Scripture, so often obscured by reading in verses or short fragments. For the professed student of literature it has the further purpose of discussing methodically such literary forms as epic, lyric, dramatic, etc., so far as they appear in one of the world's great literatures. It assumes that the English Bible is a supreme classic, the thorough study of which must form a part of all liberal education.

CONTENTS:

INTRODUCTION: The *Book of Job*, and the various kinds of literary interest represented by it. BOOK I: First Principles of Literary classification illustrated from Sacred Literature. BOOK II: Lyric Poetry of the Bible. BOOK III: Biblical History and Epic. BOOK IV: The Philosophy of the Bible, or Wisdom Literature. BOOK V: Biblical Literature of Prophecy. BOOK VI: Biblical Literature of Rhetoric. APPENDIX: Tables intended as a manual for Bible reading from the literary point of view. *[Ready in April.*

History and Literature in Grammar Grades.

By J. H. PHILLIPS, Superintendent Public Schools, Birmingham, Ala. Paper. 19 pages. Retail price, 15 cents. (Monographs on Education Series.)

DISCUSSES past and present methods of teaching these branches, and suggests improvements.

American Literature.

An Elementary Text-Book for use in High Schools and Colleges. By JULIAN HAWTHORNE and LEONARD LEMMON, Supt. of Schools, Sherman, Texas. Cloth. Illustrated. 319 pages. Introduction price, $1.12. Price by mail, $1.25.

THIS book is prepared in the light of modern methods of teaching literature. No other volume approaches it in the number and value of its poetical selections from copyrighted matter. These selections are taken from our best known poets; and, appended, are studies of these selections and of the authors' whole product; and as these exercises are new in this kind of volume they will undoubtedly be warmly welcomed by teachers.

The authors have taken special pains with the grouping and arrangement of the volume, and have tried to make the book an organic, living structure; to make the authors treated appear as living persons to the pupils; to give the pupil a comprehension of the nature of the authors' mind and genius, of what they tried to accomplish and how near they came to accomplishing it. They have tried to keep the pupil reminded, concurrently, of the general historical situation during the various literary periods, and how the literature was affected thereby; and of the political or other references that aided to give bias and tone to literary productions. The book aims to stimulate the pupil's thought rather than tax his memory. [*Send for our special circular.*]

James R. Truax, *Prof. of English Language and Literature, Union College, N.Y.*: It is refreshing to find a work like this that exhibits a just idea of proportion. This book is a valuable guide to those in search of the best in literature.

J. M. Greenwood, *Supt. Pub. Schs., Kansas City, Mo.*: It contains more solid sense to the square inch on American authors than all the other books written in this country.

W. S. Eversole, *Supt. Public Schools, Wooster, O.*: It is a thoroughly interesting and stimulating book.

London Literary World: It is more than a school book: it is in itself a valuable addition to American literature.

A. K. Goudy, *State Supt., Nebraska:* The book is certainly one deserving commendation and is highly appreciated by this department and will receive personal recommendations to our teachers.

C. A. Whiting, *Prof. of Literature, University of Deseret, Salt Lake City:* I think it the finest work on the subject I have ever seen.

W. C. Sawyer, *University of the Pacific, Cal.*: I find it so fresh and well adapted to an outline course that I shall use it next term.

Thos. Hume, *Univ. of North Carolina:* I have been the means of having it used by a class of eighty-four preparatory students.

ENGLISH LITERATURE.

Hawthorne and Lemmon's American Literature. A manual for high schools and academies. $1.25.

Meiklejohn's History of English Language and Literature. For high schools and colleges. A compact and reliable statement of the essentials; also included in Meiklejohn's English Language (see under English Language). 90 cts.

Meiklejohn's History of English Literature. 116 pages. Part IV of English Literature, above. 45 cts.

Hodgkins' Studies in English Literature. Gives full lists of aids for laboratory method. Scott, Lamb, Wordsworth, Coleridge, Byron, Shelley, Keats, Macaulay, Dickens, Thackeray, Robert Browning, Mrs. Browning, Carlyle, George Eliot, Tennyson, Rossetti, Arnold, Ruskin, Irving, Bryant, Hawthorne, Longfellow, Emerson, Whittier, Holmes, and Lowell. A separate pamphlet on each author. Price 5 cts. each, or per hundred, $3.00; complete in cloth (adjustable file cover, $1.50). $1.00.

Scudder's Shelley's Prometheus Unbound. With introduction and copious notes. 70 cts.

George's Wordsworth's Prelude. Annotated for high school and college. Never before published alone. $1.25.

George's Selections from Wordsworth. 168 poems chosen with a view to illustrate the growth of the poet's mind and art. $1.50.

George's Wordsworth's Prefaces and Essays on Poetry. Contains the best of Wordsworth's prose. 60 cts.

George's Webster's Speeches. Nine select speeches with notes. $1.50.

George's Burke's American Orations. Cloth. 65 cts.

George's Syllabus of English Literature and History. Shows in parallel columns, the progress of History and Literature. 20 cts.

Corson's Introduction to Browning. A guide to the study of Browning's Poetry. Also has 33 poems with notes. $1.50.

Corson's Introduction to the Study of Shakespeare. A critical study of Shakespeare's art, with examination questions. $1.50.

Corson's Introduction to the Study of Milton. *In press.*

Corson's Introduction to the Study of Chaucer. *In press.*

Cook's Judith. The Old English epic poem, with introduction, translation, glossary and fac-simile page. $1.60. Students' edition without translation. 35 cts.

Cook's The Bible and English Prose Style. Approaches the study of the Bible from the literary side. 60 cts.

Simonds' Sir Thomas Wyatt and his Poems. 168 pages. With biography, and critical analysis of his poems. 75 cts.

Hall's Beowulf. A metrical translation. $1.00. Students' edition. 35 cts.

Norton's Heart of Oak Books. A series of five volumes giving selections from the choicest English literature.

Phillips's History and Literature in Grammar Grades. An essay showing the intimate relation of the two subjects. 15 cts.

See also our list of books for the study of the English Language.

D. C. HEATH & CO., PUBLISHERS.
BOSTON.   NEW YORK.   CHICAGO.

ENGLISH LANGUAGE.

Hyde's Lessons in English, Book I. For the lower grades. Contains exercises for reproduction, picture lessons, letter writing, *uses* of parts of speech, etc. 40 cts.

Hyde's Lessons in English, Book II. For Grammar schools. Has enough technical grammar for correct use of language. 60 cts.

Hyde's Lessons in English, Book II with Supplement. Has, in addition to the above, 118 pages of technical grammar. 70 cts. Supplement bound alone, 35 cts.

Hyde's Advanced Lessons in English. For advanced classes in grammar schools and high schools. 60 cts.

Hyde's Lessons in English, Book II with Advanced Lessons. The Advanced Lessons and Book II bound together. 80 cts.

Hyde's Derivation of Words. 15 cts.

Mathews's Outline of English Grammar, with Selections for Practice. The application of principles is made through composition of original sentences. 80 cts.

Buckbee's Primary Word Book. Embraces thorough drills in articulation and in the primary difficulties of spelling and sound. 30 cts.

Sever's Progressive Speller. For use in advanced primary, intermediate, and grammar grades. Gives spelling, pronunciation, definition, and use of words. 30 cts.

Badlam's Suggestive Lessons in Language. Being Part I and Appendix of Suggestive Lessons in Language and Reading. 50 cts.

Smith's Studies in Nature, and Language Lessons. A combination of object lessons with language work. 50 cts. Part I bound separately, 25 cts.

Meiklejohn's English Language. Treats salient features with a master's skill and with the utmost clearness and simplicity. $1.30.

Meiklejohn's English Grammar. Also composition, versification, paraphrasing, etc. For high schools and colleges. 90 cts.

Meiklejohn's History of the English Language. 78 pages. Part III of English Language above, 35 cts.

Williams's Composition and Rhetoric by Practice. For high school and college. Combines the smallest amount of theory with an abundance of practice. Revised edition. $1.00.

Strang's Exercises in English. Examples in Syntax, Accidence, and Style for criticism and correction. 50 cts.

Huffcutt's English in the Preparatory School. Presents as practically as possible some of the advanced methods of teaching English grammar and composition in the secondary schools. 25 cts.

Woodward's Study of English. Discusses English teaching from primary school to high collegiate work. 25 cts.

Genung's Study of Rhetoric. Shows the most practical discipline of students for the making of literature. 25 cts.

Goodchild's Book of Stops. Punctuation in Verse. Illustrated. 10 cts.

See also our list of books for the study of English Literature.

D. C. HEATH & CO., PUBLISHERS,
BOSTON.   NEW YORK.   CHICAGO.

www.ingramcontent.com/pod-product-compliance
Lightning Source LLC
Chambersburg PA
CBHW022147160426
43197CB00009B/1455